A WORLD BANK COUNTRY STUDY

Poland's Labor Market

The Challenge of Job Creation

The World Bank
Washington, D.C.

Contents

Tables

Figures

Boxes

ABSTRACT

This study reviews recent labor market developments in Poland, examining the factors behind the rise in unemployment and proposing actions that could contribute toward increasing the rate of job creation. The study has been prepared in collaboration with and based on extensive discussion the World Bank team had with the Government of Poland, and in particular with the Ministry of Labor and Social Policy. The team also had productive discussions with representatives of trade unions and employers. The main purpose of the study is therefore to inform – based on research findings – the policy discussion on the labor market that currently takes place in Poland.

The study has two main findings:

- The recent rise in unemployment results primarily from an acceleration of job destruction that began with the wave of enterprise restructuring in the aftermath of the Russia crisis, and has persisted in part because of an imbalance in the fiscal-monetary policy mix. While the acceleration of job destruction has been accompanied by an increase in job creation, the jobs being created differ in a salient way from the jobs being destroyed. There are differences in the location of these new jobs and in the skills required from workers. Most of the new jobs have been created in the service sector within the Warsaw area, and many of these jobs require better educated workers. Another significant feature about this restructuring of the Polish labor market is that the private sector is driving the process. The private sector creates annually over twice as many jobs (relative to its employment) than the public sector, and almost half of the new jobs are being created by business start-ups.

- The recent rise in unemployment has highlighted important barriers in the transition from old to new jobs. These include a binding minimum wage, high taxes on labor income, limitations in the labor code, and a relatively easy access to early retirement and other social benefits. Some individuals that fall into unemployment find that living on social transfers (social assistance, family benefits, unemployment benefits, etc.) is preferable to working at the minimum wage, losing benefits, and paying taxes. There are, however, high social and fiscal costs associated with these so-called unemployment and underemployment traps. Workers that received unemployment benefits for extended periods have greater difficulties in re-entering the labor market. Early withdrawals from the labor force through early retirement, and widespread abuse of disability pensions, have resulted in a heavy burden on current contributors to the social security system, with the system's old age dependency ratio (pensioners to contributors) rising to 67 percent in 2000, up from 43 percent in 1990.

PREFACE

The study is based on the research findings and interviews conducted by the World Bank team working on Poland in the second half of 2000. The team wishes to thank the Government of Poland for the excellent cooperation received from its senior government officials in the Ministry of Labor and Social Policy, the National Labor Office, and the Central Statistical Office. The team also wishes to thank Government officials, members of Parliament, academics, representatives of the Federation of Employers, and representatives of the trade unions OPZZ and Solidarity for productive discussions with the team.

The preliminary findings of this study were first presented to an audience of interested parties in Poland at a conference held in Warsaw on May 9, 2001. The conference included as panelists and participants many of those consulted during the preparation of the study -- Government officials, members of Parliament, academics, representatives of the Federation of Employers, and representatives of the trade unions OPPZ and Solidarity. The conference provided the opportunity for those consulted to present their views on findings of the study. While there was not full agreement on all issues discussed, the conference was an important input to the preparation of the final draft of this report. The World Bank team would like to thank the conference's panelists and participants for sharing their thoughts and for helping make the preparation and completion of this study an open and consultative process.

Carlos Cavalcanti was the principal author of the study, drawing from background papers and contributions prepared by a team composed by Mmes. Alejandra Cox-Edwards, Maryla Maliszewska, and Irena Topinska, and Messrs. Ryszard Petru, Marcin Przybyla, Hernan Fuenzalida-Puelma, and Jan Rutkowski. The study benefited from the constructive criticism of the peer reviewers – Messrs. Peter Fallon and Thomas Hoopengardner -- and comments from Ms. Christine Jones, and Messrs. Michael Carter, Terry Cochran (EC), Bernard Funck, Patrick Lenain (OECD), Kyle Peters, Michal Rutkowski, Abebe Selassie (IMF), Graham Smith, and John Strongman.

The team gratefully acknowledges the assistance of several World Bank colleagues. Mr. Jacek Wojciechowicz organized the dissemination of the findings of this study. Ms. Malgorzata Chacinska organized the team's visits to Poland and the conference where the findings of this study were presented. Ms. Anita Correa provided superb assistance in the processing of this study.

ACRONYMS AND ABBREVIATIONS

EPL	Employment Protection Legislation
ES	Employment Services
EU	European Union
GDP	Gross Domestic Product
GUS	Polish Central Statistical Office
KRUS	Farmer's Security Fund
LLO	Local Labor Office
MNE	Ministry of National Education
NLO	National Labor Office
OECD	Organization for Economic Co-operation and Development
PLO	Powiat Labor Office
SOEs	State-Owned Enterprises
UB	Unemployment Benefit
ZUS	Social Security Fund

CURRENCY EQUIVALENTS
Currency Unit = Polish Zloty (PLN)

US$ 1 = PLN 4.20
(as of July 25, 2001)

EXECUTIVE SUMMARY

This study reviews recent labor market developments in Poland, examining the factors behind the rise in unemployment and proposing actions that could contribute toward increasing the rate of job creation. The study has been prepared in collaboration with and based on extensive discussion the World Bank team had with the Government of Poland, and in particular with the Ministry of Labor and Social Policy. The team also had productive discussions with representatives of trade unions and employers. The main purpose of the report is therefore to inform – based on research findings – the policy discussion on the labor market that currently takes place in Poland.

The study has two main findings:

- The recent rise in unemployment results primarily from an acceleration of job destruction that began with the wave of enterprise restructuring in the aftermath of the Russia crisis, and has persisted in part because of an imbalance in the fiscal-monetary policy mix. While the acceleration of job destruction has been accompanied by an increase in job creation, the jobs being created differ in a salient way from the jobs being destroyed. There are differences in the location of these new jobs and in the skills required from workers. Most of the new jobs have been created in the service sector within the Warsaw area, and many of these jobs require better educated workers. Another significant feature about this restructuring of the Polish labor market is that the private sector is driving the process. The private sector creates annually over twice as many jobs (relative to its employment) than the public sector, and almost half of the new jobs are being created by business start-ups.

- The recent rise in unemployment has highlighted important barriers in the transition from old to new jobs. These include a binding minimum wage, high taxes on labor income, limitations in the labor code, and a relatively easy access to early retirement and other social benefits. Some individuals that fall into unemployment find that living on social transfers (social assistance, family benefits, unemployment benefits, etc.) is preferable to working at the minimum wage, losing benefits, and paying taxes. There are, however, high social and fiscal costs associated with these so-called unemployment and underemployment traps. Workers that received unemployment benefits for extended periods have greater difficulties in re-entering the labor market. Early withdrawals from the labor force through early retirement, and widespread abuse of disability pensions, have resulted in a heavy burden on current contributors to the social security system, with the system's old age dependency ratio (pensioners to contributors) rising to 67 percent in 2000, up from 43 percent in 1990.

In addition, the problems with the ongoing restructuring of the Polish labor market have been compounded by an increase in new labor market entrants, primarily recent school graduates joining the labor force. The number of first time job seekers increased by almost three-quarters since 1998, compared to an increased of around 50 percent in job seekers of all ages. Although the absolute number of unemployed new labor market entrants is not particularly high (just over 20 percent), the unemployment rate among these workers below 25 is very high, reaching almost 35 percent, over twice the national average. There is a particular concern with the large share of new labor market entrants with only basic vocational education or less, especially in rural areas, since educational attainment has become an increasingly important factor in determining employment status.

Job Creation and Job Destruction

The Polish labor market has exhibited a large degree of dynamism, with a recent rise in the rates of job creation and job destruction (Figure 1). These rates of job creation and job destruction are comparable to other OECD economies, contradicting the conventional wisdom that the labor market in Poland is stagnant, and that mobility is low.

Figure 1 Gross Job Gains and Job Losses, 1993-99

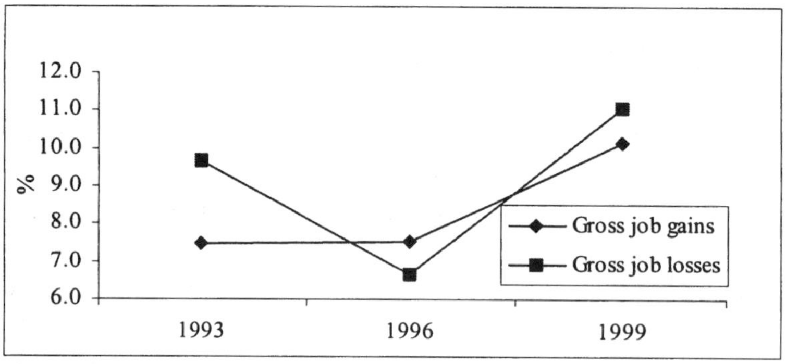

Source: Rutkowski (2001).

Where are the new jobs being created? Most of the new jobs are created in the relatively underdeveloped service economy and in industries experiencing rapid productivity growth. The latter however is also where many of the jobs have been lost. Indeed, within the manufacturing sector, most of the job flows happen between firms of the same industry, indicating that economic restructuring and job creation often go hand in hand. This also indicates that factors leading to job creation act primarily at the firm level, rather than at the industry level. Policies aimed at saving jobs at the industry level are missing, therefore, a fundamental point about the functioning of the labor market. Job creation hinges more on a favorable investment climate at the firm level than on government support to a particular industry.

What is driving the labor market restructuring? Most of the job creation has been driven by the sustained growth in domestic demand and increase access to export markets in the European Union. The latter however has only been possible because of the rapid increase in labor productivity, driven in part by increase competition from imported goods in the domestic market. While productivity growth and imports have contributed to job destruction, there are good reasons to be optimistic about the long-term effects of productivity on employment growth. While sectors experiencing rapid productivity growth, in particular manufacturing, have not accounted for a large share of net job creation, they have been responsible for many of the new jobs being created. Also, higher productivity is key for maintaining high export growth, allowing a sustained growth in domestic demand and employment.

Realizing this job growth potential will depend on several factors, including a better fiscal-monetary policy mix. The current combination of lose fiscal and tight monetary policies has lead to a weakening in domestic demand by slowing down investment, while still making foreign holdings of Zloty-denominated assets very attractive. This in turn has lead to a strong appreciation of the currency, which will eventually affect export growth. Both these developments (lower investments and slower export growth) limit the opportunities for sustained growth in employment. There is a direct effect of lowering real GDP growth, and an indirect effect of reducing long run productivity growth. The latter is key for non-inflationary wage increases. Re-establishing a virtuous cycle, whereby foreign and domestic savings are channeled back into productive investments, rather than to the financing of the budget deficit, requires priority action to meet this year's fiscal deficit target, which will in turn open room for a reduction in domestic real interest rates. This should allow a sustained recovery in investment and an eventual reversal of the recent appreciation of the Zloty. Both these developments would have a positive impact on job creation.

Barriers in the Transition from Old to New Jobs

The benefits of a better fiscal-monetary policy mix will be unevenly distributed if barriers in the transition from old to new jobs are not eliminated. While many have benefited from this dynamic labor market, finding new and better paying jobs, others have experienced increased job insecurity and lower pay. More importantly, barriers in this transition from old to new jobs still are very high, leading many people to settle for self employment or part time jobs in low productivity activities, while drawing additional income from social transfers (e.g., old age and disability pensions, unemployment benefits). For instance, 14 percent of old-age pensioners, 19 percent of disability pensioners, and 6 percent of unemployment benefit recipients report having worked in rural areas during the week of the February 1999 Labor Force survey.

Three main barriers emerge in this transition from old to new jobs:

- *Wages for less-skilled workers are set above market clearing levels*, limiting their employment and encouraging their substitution for better skilled workers earning slightly higher wages. The average difference in wages between workers with basic vocational education and workers with general secondary education is around 13 percent, reflecting the impact that the minimum wage has on setting a floor on wages for low-skilled workers. Throughout the 1990s the minimum wage was been at around 40 percent of the average wage, placing younger, less-skilled workers, especially those in less developed regions of Poland, at a particular disadvantage. As a result, workers with basic vocational education or less account for almost three-quarters of all unemployed, although they constitute only around 50 percent of the working-age population.

- *Taxes on labor income are high, accounting for 51 percent of gross wages*. This creates a wedge between labor costs and wages that both burdens employers and discourages labor supply, especially when early retirement and access to other social benefits are an option. In some instances, living on social transfers (social assistance, family benefits, unemployment benefits, etc.) is preferable to working at the minimum wage, losing benefits, and paying taxes. Calculations of marginal effective tax rate, net of cash transfers, indicate that the increase in net taxes can be as high as 120 percent for individuals moving from unemployment to a low paying job.

- *Job creation has been slow in less-developed regions.* Job creation has been very unevenly spread across Poland, leading to large regional disparities in unemployment. Comparing factors influencing the rate of job creation across the regions within Poland, the study finds that four factors accounted the most. These were (i) the size of the service sector; (ii) the share of the working age population with secondary education or more; (iii) the level of labor productivity relative to wages; and (iv) the degree of wage flexibility, especially at the lower-end of the wage distribution. The results confirm that a better educated labor force leads to higher employment, indicating that investments in education have a high payoff for both the individuals and the country. The results also corroborate the widely held view that limitations on wage adjustments at the lower-end of the wage distribution constrain job creation.

Understanding how these barriers operate, especially for less-skilled workers, is important because policymakers are always caught between providing income support to unemployed workers and finding sources of funding for these programs. Since most programs are funded through payroll taxes, this creates a vicious circle whereby programs designed to assist in labor market transitions also act as a deterrent for the creation of jobs for these same low-skilled workers.

Understanding how these barriers operate is also important because policymakers frequently express concerns about the impact of changing the minimum wage on poverty among low paid workers. This concern is overstated, however. Low paid workers account for only 3.5 percent of those in the lowest quintile (20 percent) of the expenditure distribution, compared to the 84 percent who are unemployed.[1] The poverty risk is, as expected, much higher from being unemployed than from being a low paid worker. Also, proposals aimed at raising the minimum wage will have a negligible impact on poverty. The majority of the poor are the unemployed, not low paid workers. Although measures aimed at introducing greater flexibility at the lower-end of the wage distribution might lead to a slight increase in wage inequality, it is a price worth paying to reduce an even greater inequality – poverty.

New Labor Market Entrants

While the difficulties faced by recent school graduates joining the labor force highlights the need to reduce the costs of job creation, especially the creation of first jobs, it also serves as a reminder of the need to continue investing in education and training. A part of the difficulties faced by new labor market entrants is the low level of educational attainment, hampering their chances of competing in an already very competitive labor market. Increases in educational attainment have been slow, especially in rural areas, where there is still strong reliance on vocational education.

New labor market entrants also face a binding minimum wage and limitation imposed the labor code. The incidence of minimum wage earners is higher among workers under 25 years of

---

[1] Low paid workers are defined as those earning 50 percent or less than the average earnings.

age (11 percent) than among prime-aged workers (3 percent). There are limitations on fixed-term and by-task employment contracts, which under other circumstances could provide opportunities for new labor market entrants to gain experience. The current legislation limits the cumulative duration of successive fixed-term or by-task contracts. These can only be renewed twice before being automatically transformed into contracts of indefinite duration. The government's concern is that without limitations these labor contracts would become a drain of potential social security contributions. While the issue of social security coverage is understandable, it needs to be weighed against the opportunity cost of having high unemployment among young workers, as well as the opportunity costs of funding subsidized employment programs for recent school graduates. These programs currently account for about one-fifth of all spending on active labor market programs.

The limitations on temporary contracts are particularly onerous for young women. Since employers cannot hire temporary replacement for workers on leave, such as maternity leave, there appears to be resistance on the part of employers to hiring women at child bearing age. As a result, unemployment women in the 18 to 34 age bracket account for a higher share than their share of the labor force, despite their educational attainment being on average higher than for men. Over 30 percent of women in this age group have post-secondary, vocational secondary, or general secondary education.

A Policy Agenda for Job Creation

A policy agenda for job creation needs to recognize that, while there is urgency in dealing with the unemployment problem, particularly because of its deleterious social consequences, there are no quick and easy solutions. Addressing the unemployment problem will take time, and require actions in several fronts. Some of these actions include the following:

- *Defining a better fiscal-monetary policy mix.* Undue delays in lowering official interest rates will pose a risk to domestic activity and export growth, particularly considering the recent appreciation of the Zloty. Only after some progress toward renewed fiscal consolidation is achieved, however, will the groundwork be laid for reducing real interest rates. Fiscal consolidation should result, in turn, from greater fiscal discipline at all levels, and structural reforms that reduce public spending and boost the production potential of the economy. Actions toward greater fiscal discipline includes stepping up the enforcement tax and social security payments; and enforcing a hard budget constraint on the operations of the health funds. Reforms to reduce unnecessary government spending and boost the economy's production potential include the restructuring and privatization of remaining state owned enterprises; opening energy and transport infrastructure operations (currently dominated by the state) to private investors; and improving the design of the tax system.

- *Introducing greater flexibility in the wage structure*, especially at the lower-end of the skill distribution. This can be achieved by differentiating the minimum wage either by age – setting a lower minimum wage for new labor market entrants - or by region. The argument for introducing a differentiated minimum wage is that the minimum wage is particularly binding for certain groups in the labor force (the young and the less-skilled). Indeed, while the minimum wage is set at around 40 percent of the average wage, it is equivalent to 65 percent of the median wage for young workers and 72 percent of the median wage for workers in elementary occupations. In some of the most depressed regions of the country, such as Slupskie, Wloclawskie and Ciechanowskie, the national minimum wage accounts for well over 90 percent of the median wage for workers in the lower 20 percent of the wage distribution. In Slupskie, for instance, workers in the lowest 20 percent of the wage distribution earn on average only 3 percent more than the national minimum wage, indicating that many low-skilled workers in Slupskie could have been employed if there were a regional differentiation of the minimum wage. While this differentiation might lead to an increase in wage inequality, it is a price worth paying to avoid an even greater inequality – inequality in the access to jobs.

- *Reducing taxes on labor income,* lowering the cost of job creation. The single most important non-wage labor cost in Poland are the taxes on labor income, which include the personal income tax and payroll taxes. This high tax wedge contributes toward reducing labor supply by encouraging eligible workers to withdraw from the labor market. Also, this wedge between labor costs and wages discourages labor demand, especially of less-skilled workers, further contributing to the slow expansion of formal employment in the economy. While steps to reduce the tax wedge on labor have been taken by re-organizing the pension system, aligning benefits and contributions more closely, and by tightening the rules on sickness allowances, more still needs to be done. Options to reduce the tax on labor income include increasing the flat income tax deduction for the personal income tax and income tax credits for low income tax families with one working adult. Options to reduce the payroll tax will depend on efforts to (i) identify sources other than payroll taxes to fund active labor market programs; (ii) eliminate the implicit 2.4 percent payroll tax designed to encourage the employment of workers with disabilities; and (iii) continue curbing the abuse of early retirement, disability and sickness benefits.

- *Proceeding with proposed changes in the labor code.* These proposals include revisions of labor market legislation concerning temporary contracts, substitute employees, employment in firms with less than 50 employees and payment for overtime work. In most instances, these revisions are designed to bring the labor code up to date with modern practices, aligning the legislation with the needs of the emerging service sector. There is scope to proceed with these revisions without compromising workers basic rights. This will require, however, that no more than a certain number (e.g., three) fix-term or by-task contracts take place with intervals between contracts of less than one month. It will also require attention to the forms of remuneration under these contracts. These should all be taxable, avoiding the risk that employers combine minimum wages and other means of compensation to not pay payroll taxes and social security contributions. Finally, the payment for overtime work in Poland should be standardized at 50 percent over the payment for regular hours, with a limit on overtime to a maximum of 4 hours a day. This is the standard in most OECD countries.

- *Investing in worker's education and training.* This includes improving access and the quality of education and training, especially in rural areas. This in turn requires further progress in moving away from vocational education programs, emphasizing instead general education that provides skills that are broader, transferable, and in greater demand. Actions to complete this transition can be aided by the introduction of a national learning assessment. This should help guide policymakers in monitoring quality and in allocating funds across educational programs and regions, targeting those in greatest need. In training programs, emphasis should be given to programs that target particular problems (e.g., skills in short supply), and individuals whose problems are clearly identified and only moderately severe.

- *Re-aligning the incentives under labor market programs.* The incentives under labor market programs encourage workers to continue drawing on unemployment benefits until the end of the eligibility period; compel older workers to remain in high unemployment areas; and lead training program administrators to target workers that have a better chance of finding a job upon graduation. Actions to re-align the incentives under these programs include the following: (i) giving re-employment bonuses to workers who find a job before ending their first six months on unemployment benefits; (ii) tightening the eligibility to pre-retirement benefits to eligible unemployed workers over 60; and (iii) targeting active labor market programs toward individuals likely to be caught in unemployment and underemployment traps – less-skilled workers, youth, the disabled, and workers in high unemployment areas. Re-employment bonuses should increase job search effort before the end of the unemployment benefit period, reducing unemployment duration. Tighter eligibility criteria for pre-retirement benefits should discourage workers from high unemployment areas from staying behind to become eligible. Targeting training programs toward unemployed workers at greater risk of remaining unemployed mitigates the risks of structural unemployment.

- *Lowering the costs of starting and running businesses.* Since most new jobs are created in the private sector, and almost half of the new jobs are created by business start ups, actions to lower the costs of starting and running businesses would have a high payoff. These actions include (i) establishing a transparent business environment that is free of undue privilege and administrative discretion; (ii) simplifying the tax system; and (iii) setting high standards in public administration services. A structurally deficient public administration increases the cost of regulatory and tax compliance that are impediments to the development of the Polish private sector, as well as to attracting needed FDI inflows.

While this policy agenda is broad, and will take time to implement, the challenge for Polish policymakers is to seize the opportunity created by the intense restructuring the labor market is currently undergoing to implement this agenda. Attention should focus on facilitating job creation, rather than stopping job destruction. Job creation can be achieved by reducing the costs of creating new jobs, aligning the labor code to the needs of the emerging service sector, and investing in worker's education and training, especially in the rural areas. This should allow the labor market to enter a virtuous cycle, whereby workers move towards growing industries, helping support increases in productivity and, in doing so, sustain high rates of economic growth. Attempts to stop job destruction will only delay job reallocation, slowing down productivity and economic growth, and raising even further unemployment among less-skilled workers. Every job saved in the State sector is paid for by slower job creation in the private sector. State sector jobs entail either higher public sector spending, or forgone tax revenues, increasing the public sector deficit and keeping real interest rates high. Also, early withdraws from the labor force through early retirement or abuse of disability pensions limit the scope for reducing the perceived tax element of social security contributions, burdening employers and discouraging labor supply.

CHAPTER 1. INTRODUCTION AND RECENT DEVELOPMENTS

After several years of declining unemployment rates, unemployment in Poland began rising again in early 1999. By December 1999, the unemployment rate had reached levels comparable to 1993, when the economy was still in the early stages of the post-transformation recovery. By the first quarter of 2000, the labor force survey measure of unemployment reached its highest level on record (16.7 percent), remaining in the 15 to 16 percent range in the following quarters (Figure 1.1).[2] Unemployment rose in every region of the country and among every group within the labor market. The highest increase in unemployment was among workers that had previously been less affected -- middle aged males in urban areas. This included workers from regions where unemployment had been relatively low in the recent past, such as Śląskie, where unemployment doubled in three years, reaching a high of 17 percent by the second half of 2000. Another important group were recent school graduate joining the labor force. A large inflow of new labor market entrants in the fall of 1999 increased youth unemployment even further, reaching one in every three workers less than 25 years old. Meanwhile, unemployment among female workers and workers with lower educational attainment continued to rise from already very high levels. Workers with basic vocational education or less saw their unemployment rate rise by around 60 percent between end-1997 and end-2000 (Table 1.1).

Figure 1.1 Unemployment Rates, May 1992/Dec. 2000

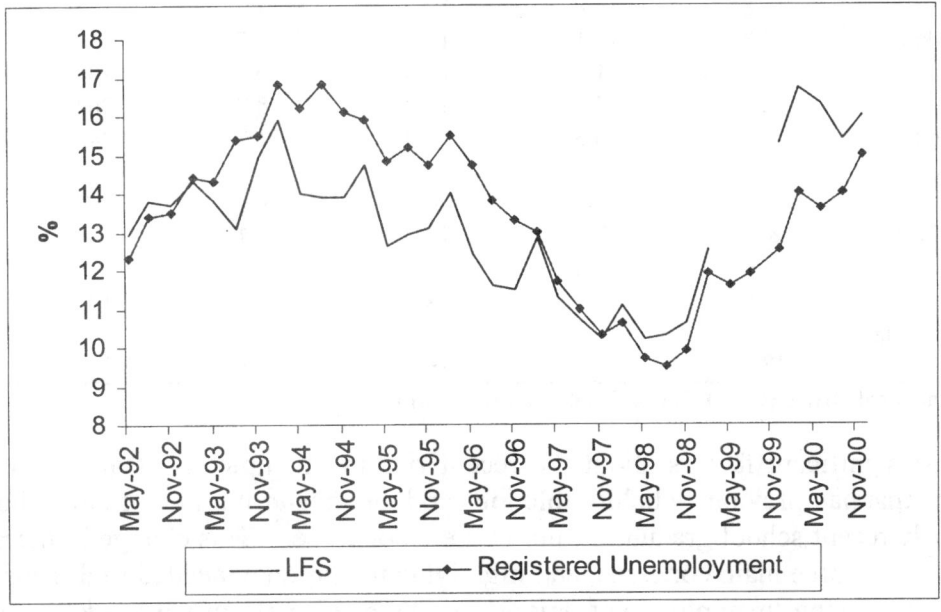

Source: Central Statistical Office (GUS). World Bank Staff calculations.

---

[2] The difference between the data reported by labor force survey and the data from the labor offices is that the former is based on a representative survey of work activity in a given week, while the labor office registration data is based on self-reporting by the individuals and tends to reflect incentives to register. The interruption in the time series from the labor force survey between February and November 1999 was due to changes in the periodicity of the survey and did not entail any changes in methodology.

Table 1.1 Unemployment Trends, 1997-2000 (%)

	1997	1998	1999	2000		1997 to 2000
	November		4th quarter	3rd quarter	4th Quarter	% Change
Total unemployment	10.2	10.6	15.3	15.4	16.0	56.9
Males	8.7	9.3	13.0	13.6	14.2	**63.2**
Females	12.0	12.2	18.1	17.5	18.1	50.8
Urban areas	10.7	11.1	13.8	16.6	16.9	**57.9**
Rural areas	9.3	9.9	11.7	13.3	14.3	53.8
LT unemployment	4.5	4.3	5.9	6.1	6.6	46.7
By age groups						
15-24	23.2	23.3	32.5	33.2	34.1	47.0
25-34	10.2	10.6	15.6	15.5	16.2	58.8
35-44	8.9	9.1	12.2	12.7	13.2	48.3
45 and over	5.8	6.9	10.4	10.3	10.7	**84.5**
By voivodships:						
Małopolskie	9.2	8.1	14.0	11.6	11.5	25.0
Mazowieckie	8.4	9.2	12.6	12.7	12.8	52.4
Wielkopolskie	7.0	7.5	13.2	12.8	13.2	88.6
Lubelskie	7.7	8.2	13.7	13.8	13.3	72.7
Podlaskie	9.7	9.8	12.8	13.8	14.0	44.3
Opolskie	10.5	11.4	13.8	16.3	15.1	43.8
Swiętokrzyskie	10.4	13.1	16.2	13.4	15.3	47.1
Pomorskie	10.4	11.1	17.0	14.8	16.9	62.5
Sląskie	8.3	10.2	14.5	17.2	17.0	**104.8**
Lódzkie	11.3	10.7	14.6	16.9	17.1	51.3
Kujawsko-pomorskie	12.4	12.2	15.9	18.9	17.5	41.1
Podkarpackie	11.8	11.8	17.4	14.7	17.9	51.7
Zachodniopomorskie	14.8	15.1	19.0	17.7	18.5	25.0
Lubuskie	11.1	11.8	19.0	20.2	20.7	86.5
Dolnośląskie	12.7	13.3	18.2	18.9	20.9	64.6
Warmińsko-Mazurskie	18.5	16.8	24.0	21.7	24.0	29.7
By education level:						
Tertiary	2.0	3.0	4.8	5.5	4.8	140.0
Vocational secondary	8.9	8.6	13.0	13.1	13.6	52.8
General secondary	13.0	13.5	19.2	18.6	19.6	50.8
Basic vocational	12.0	12.5	18.4	18.1	19.2	**60.0**
Primary and incomplete primary	12.5	14.4	19.2	19.8	20.2	**61.6**

Source: Central Statistical Office (GUS). World Bank staff calculations.

The most significant factors about the recent rise in unemployment are the increasing share of workers that had previously held stable jobs and the greater number of new labor market entrants, primarily recent school graduates joining the labor force.[3] This change in the profile of unemployment raises three main concerns, and highlights the urgency needed in dealing with the problem. First, the rising unemployment among middle-aged male urban workers signals the

---

[3] In addition, there are discouraged workers, who have registered as unemployed to take advantage of new administrative rules. These new rule are the health insurance legislation requiring unemployed to register to remain covered, and the January 2000 transfer of labor offices to local authorities. The transfer lead labor office managers to encourage registration because their budgets are determined in part through a formula that assigns weights to the number of registered unemployed in their jurisdiction.

intense restructuring the labor market is undergoing, with jobs being created and destroyed at a rate seen only before during the early years of economic transformation. The main difference this time is the private sector is driving the restructuring process. Solutions to the unemployment problem need therefore to reflect this dominant role played by the private sector. This includes aligning the labor code to the needs of the emerging service sector, facilitating the transition from lifetime, full-time employment in industrial settings to flextime employment in the service sector, without compromising worker's basic rights. It also includes bringing more private sector workers into collective agreements by decentralizing wage bargaining procedures, and setting age-specific and regional thresholds for the minimum wage.

Second, the rapid rise in unemployment signals the exhaustion of many of the established unemployment buffers: withdrawals from the labor force through early retirement and underemployment in rural areas. Early withdrawals from the labor force through early retirement, and widespread abuse of disability pensions, have resulted in a heavy burden on current contributors to the welfare system, with the system's old age dependency ratio (pensioners to contributors) rising to 67 percent in 2000, up from 43 percent in 1990. Underemployment in agriculture is no longer an option for displaced industrial workers, since there is already widespread unemployment (open and hidden) in rural areas, with the sector employing almost 20 percent of the labor force, while accounting for less than 5 percent of GDP. While this exhaustion of unemployment buffers reflects their increase fiscal burden, it also makes more evident the link between poverty and unemployment. Between 1996 and 1999 the risk of falling into poverty as a result of being unemployed rose from three to four times. This result places greater urgency on better targeting government transfers toward the poor, and to introducing incentives to reduce the time unemployed workers spend in labor market programs. There is ample evidence of increase dependency on unemployment benefits and other government transfers, leading to so-called unemployment traps, whereby individuals at the margin of the labor market alternate periods receiving unemployment benefits and other government transfers with periods of informal employment or underemployment.

Third, the difficulties faced by recent school graduates joining the labor force highlight the need to reduce the costs of job creation, especially the creation of first jobs, and to continue investing in education and training. This will allow new labor market entrants to better compete in this already very competitive labor market. Recent school graduates face a variety of barriers in their entry to the labor market. The taxes on labor income are high (51 percent of gross wages), creating a wedge between labor costs and wages that limit job creation. Also, the minimum wage in Poland is high relative to the average wage (40 percent), placing less-skilled new entrants in a disadvantaged position. Finally, there are limitations on fixed-term and by-task employment contracts, which under other circumstances could provide opportunities for new labor market entrants to gain experience. These problems are compounded by the slow increase in educational attainment. A majority of the new labor market entrants who are unemployed (54 percent) has only primary and vocational education or less. Action to reduce the costs of job creation include reducing payroll taxes; making the minimum wage less binding for younger, less-skilled workers, especially in high unemployment areas; and eliminating constraints on the expansion of fixed-term and by-task labor contracts. It also includes actions to improve education and training, especially in rural areas.

The rest of this introduction elaborates on this new profile of unemployment, one where there is a greater participation of workers from enterprises undergoing restructuring, an increase in school graduates joining the labor force, and a return of discouraged unemployed workers no longer eligible for government transfers. It begins by identifying recent unemployment trends. Who is joining the ranks of the unemployed? What is the duration of their unemployment? How does unemployment duration vary with the age, gender, and educational attainment? What is the link between unemployment and poverty? Next, it turns to factors magnifying these recent labor market developments: the increase in the number of labor market entrants, the rising skills mismatch; and the limitations imposed by the labor market legislation. The introduction closes with a presentation of what lies ahead, outlining what is discussed in the other chapters of this study.

Who is joining the ranks of the unemployed? Two groups account for the majority of those joining the ranks of unemployment: workers from enterprises undergoing restructuring and less- skilled youth from the new generation of baby boomers joining the workforce. In addition, there are discouraged workers who have registered as unemployed to take advantage of new administrative rules. This includes health insurance legislation requiring unemployed to register to remain covered, and the January 2000 transfer of labor offices to local authorities. This transfer lead labor office managers to encourage registration because their budgets are determined in part through a formula that assigns weights to the number of registered unemployed in their jurisdiction.[4]

Enterprise restructuring. A large and growing share of workers joining the unemployment ranks are workers leaving enterprises undergoing restructuring (Table 1.2). This includes middle-aged male workers in industrialized areas that have traditionally been less affected by unemployment (e.g., Slaskie). Most layoffs have been in the private sector, especially in manufacturing, reflecting a wave of enterprise restructuring following the Russia crisis and increase penetration of Western imports into the domestic market. The labor restructuring programs in large state owned enterprises (steel, coal, and defense industries), while still important, account for a smaller share of actual layoffs because many of those leaving these industries opted for early retirement.

Table 1.2 Worker's Reasons for Leaving Previous Job, 1997-2000 (thousand)

	Quarterly Average 1997	Quarterly Average 1998	1st Quarter 1999	4th Quarter 1999	1st Quarter 2000	Percentage Change: 1st Quarter 2000/ Quarterly Average 1998
Retirement	129	137	149	211	188	37.7
Enterprise restructuring	**634**	**589**	**735**	**909**	**1,025**	**73.9**
Dismissed for other reasons	150	139	167	200	222	60.3
Finished temporary job	312	273	333	295	374	36.9
Other reasons	338	322	357	430	466	44.7
Total	1,563	1,460	1,741	2,045	2,275	55.9

Source: Central Statistical Agency; Labor Force Survey (several). World Bank staff calculations.

---

[4] While it is difficult to quantify precisely the effect of these new administrative rules on the number of registered unemployed, it appears that it has encouraged many people working in the informal sector, as well as discouraged workers, to register as unemployed. This in turn is reflected in the labor force survey, since people who register as unemployed also tend to identify themselves as unemployed to surveyors.

This new round of layoffs raised immediate concern because many of the established buffers to absorb unemployment have now been exhausted. During the 1990s, most of the decline in unemployment was associated with a reduction in labor force participation through early retirement programs and displaced industrial workers returning to under-employment in rural areas.[5] These options of early withdrawal from the labor market and a return of displaced industrial workers to rural areas are no longer sustainable, however. Early withdrawals from the labor force through early retirement, and widespread abuse of disability pensions, have resulted in a heavy burden on current contributors to the welfare system. The system's old age dependency ratio (pensioners to contributors) reached 67 percent in 2000, up from 43 percent in 1990. The average retirement age was 59 for men and 55 for women, compared to the eligibility age of 65 for men and 60 for women. The number of disability pensioners per thousand labor force participants is very high, 153,[6] compared to 100 in Hungary and Latvia, countries with similar disability systems before the transition.[7] The recently established pre-retirement benefits have also ran into financial difficulties because requests for these benefits last year greatly exceeded the funding available from payroll taxes. Finally, agriculture can no longer provide alternative employment for displaced industrial workers. There is already widespread unemployment (open and hidden) in rural areas, with the sector employing almost 20 percent of the labor force, while accounting for less than 5 percent of GDP.

Unemployment duration. The exhaustion of these unemployment buffers are reflected in the recent increase in the duration of unemployment (Figure 1.2). After declining from a 20 month average in early 1994 to around 10 months in late 1998, unemployment duration began rising again in late 1999, almost reverting back to the 1994 highs in the Spring of 2000. Moreover, the duration of unemployment is now highest for those in greatest difficulty of finding new jobs once they become unemployed: older and less-skilled workers. Data for 1999 indicates that the two most important factors leading to higher unemployment duration are educational attainment and age. Unemployment duration rises the lower the educational attainment of the worker, reaching an all time high of 15 months for workers with basic vocational education or less.[8] This is consistent with the fact that unemployment rates are higher for workers with lower educational attainment. Unemployment duration also rises with age, reaching an average of 16 months for workers over 45. This is in contrast with what happens to workers with lower educational attainment, however, because older workers usually have lower unemployment rates.

---

[5] For instance, between 1994 and 1998 Katowice lost 25,000 jobs in basic metals manufacturing, while still keeping its position as Poland's largest urban agglomeration. It also managed to keep unemployment low, 7.8 percent compared to the country's average of 12.3 percent for this period. Where did displaced manufacturing workers go? While Katowice had strong growth in finance and business services, the fastest growing sectors was agriculture, adding 20,000 jobs between 1994 to 1998.

[6] ZUS figures indicate 2.7 million disability beneficiaries of all ages, which is more than 200 per thousand. To make this figure comparable to other countries, World Bank staff estimates have scaled back this figure by 23 percent to reflect that disability pensions do not automatically turn into old-age pensions when beneficiaries reach pension age, as in other countries.

[7] Not surprisingly, a survey conducted by the Central Statistical Office (GUS) in 1996 reported that almost one third of those at working age legally certified to receive disability benefits did not consider themselves disabled.

[8] It is important to note that this is a lower bound estimate for unemployment duration because it is based on the ratio between the stock of unemployed and the inflow into unemployment. When unemployment rises, the ratio drops because those joining the ranks of the unemployed have, at that given moment in time, lower unemployment spells.

This suggests that, while older workers are less likely to become unemployed, they are also less likely to find a new job once they become unemployed.[9]

Figure 1.2 Average Duration of Unemployment (in months) March 1993/2000

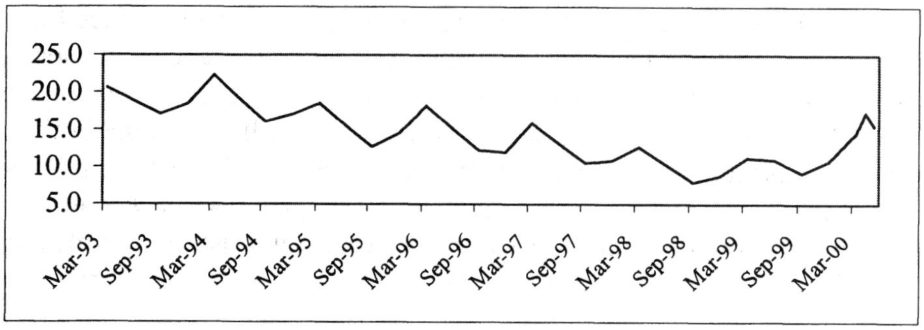

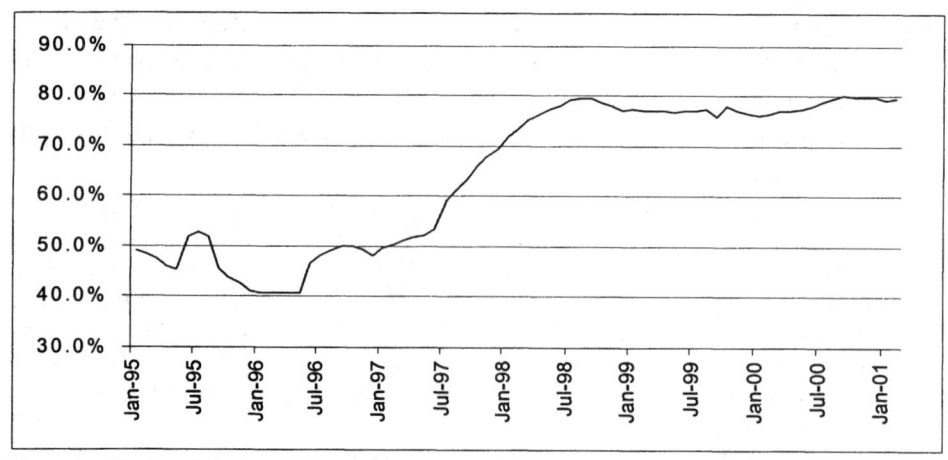

Source: National Labor Office

Coverage of unemployment benefits. The concern about the increase in the duration of unemployment needs to be reflected, among other places, in the policies regarding coverage of unemployment benefits. Today only about 20 percent of registered unemployed are entitled to unemployment benefits (Figure 1.3),[10] down from about 50 percent in early 1997. This reduced coverage of unemployment benefits reflects the tightening of eligibility criteria that began in the second half of 1997, which aimed at increasing the targeting of unemployment benefits to the poor.   Indeed, while unemployment benefits are not formally means-tested, coverage of unemployment benefits reaches 50 percent of the registered unemployed in the bottom 10 percent (first decile) of the income distribution, compared to 25 percent of those in the entire universe of registered unemployed. This improved targeting becomes a problem however when there is a sudden increase in unemployment, especially if there is a shift in the profile of unemployed.

Figure 1.3 Registered Unemployed without Benefits (%)

Source: National Labor Office

---

[9] The other two factors influencing unemployment duration are gender and place of residence. Unemployment duration is higher for female than for male workers, and higher for rural than for urban workers, with these two factors increasing the average unemployment duration of 12.5 months by 10 to 15 percent.

[10] Although within this one-quarter of registered unemployed targeting is quite effective, with over 50 percent of the registered unemployed in the first decile receiving unemployment benefits.

Poverty and unemployment. The recent increase in unemployment has highlighted the ever closer link between unemployment and the risks of falling into poverty. While those with employment income or income tied to wages (pensioners) were best able to avoid the risk of falling into poverty, the unemployed, those living on unproductive agricultural holdings, and those outside the labor force (children, the disabled and other dependents) faced a much higher risk of falling into poverty. Estimates for 1999 indicate that 30 percent of households living in the bottom 20 percent (quintile) of the expenditure distribution had at least one unemployed member. This percentage increased to 40 percent for households living in the bottom 10 percent (decile) of the income distribution. Also, the unemployed and those living in unproductive agricultural holding faced a risk four times higher of falling into poverty than those living in households with at least one member employed. This is up from a risk three times higher during the period 1993 to 1996.[11]

Policies for job creation are an important element in a strategy to help individuals either avoid, or exit from, poverty. This holds true even if creating job opportunities for less-skilled workers requires greater flexibility at the lower-end of the wage distribution. Indeed, policymakers frequently express concerns about the impact of changes in the minimum wage on poverty among low paid workers. This concern is overstated, however. Low paid workers account for only 3.5 percent of those living in the lowest quintile (20 percent) of the expenditure distribution, compared to the 84 percent who are unemployed.[12] This finding is important because it indicates that the poverty risk is, as expected, much higher from being unemployed than from being a low paid worker. It also indicates that proposals aimed at raising the minimum wage will have a negligible impact on poverty. The majority of the poor are the unemployed, not low paid workers. Although measures aimed at introducing greater flexibility at the lower-end of the wage distribution might lead to a slight increase in wage inequality, it is a price worth paying to reduce an even greater inequality – poverty.[13]

New labor market entrants. These pressures on the labor market caused by economic restructuring and the exhaustion of unemployment buffers are magnified by the increase in the number of new labor market entrants, primarily recent school graduates joining the workforce. While the number of job searchers increased by around one half between the first half of 1998 and the first quarter of 2000, the number of first time job seekers increased by almost three-

---

[11] Estimates for 1999 are based on the Polish household budget survey (PHBS) conducted by Central Statistical Office in 1999. The sample includes over 30,000 households (31,428), or over 100,000 individuals. Every household has been surveyed for one month, so in fact, the sample consists of 12 monthly sub-samples of fairly equal size (over 2,500 each). It is representative for entire population, excluding those living abroad or outside 'standard' households (in dormitories, for instance). Estimates for the period 1994 to 1996 are reported in Okrasa (1999) and are based on a four-year panel data constructed from Poland's Household Budget Survey. To build the panel, however, Okrasa (1999) excluded households that changed residential address during the four year period under analysis.

[12] Low paid workers are defined as those earning 50 percent or less than the average earnings. While the share of low paid workers in the lowest quintile (20 percent) of the expenditure distribution rises to 6 percent when one considers only the working age population, this is still much lower than the 71 percent of the poor who are also unemployed in this age group.

[13] While women earn on average 18 percent less than men with similar characteristics, they don't face a greater of poverty because of low wages. Indeed, low paid men face a slightly higher risk of poverty (25 percent) than women (24 percent). This reflects two factors. Low paid women are usually the second income earners in the household. Also, gender differences in earnings usually reveal themselves in the higher earnings categories.

quarters during this same period (Table 1.3). Unsurprisingly, the unemployment rate among workers below 25 is now over two times the national average. This increase in numbers of new entrants reflects demographic pressures from baby boomers joining the workforce and is expected to persist for the next several years. The number of new labor market entrants is projected to continue increasing by around 800,000 for the next four years before falling to around 400,000 in the 2004-2008 period.

Table 1.3 Worker's Reason for Job Search, 1997-2000 (thousand)

	1st Half 1997	2nd Half 1997	1st Half 1998	2nd Half 1998	1st Quarter 1999	4th Quarter 1999	1st Quarter 2000	% change: 1Q 2000/1H 1998
Loss of job	1,140	936	946	930	1,169	1,333	1,518	50.9
Resignation	153	138	141	121	153	130	176	25.7
Return to work	405	356	400	384	418	583	581	44.5
Start first job	**353**	**366**	**339**	**373**	**401**	**595**	**604**	**73.6**
Total	2,051	1,795	1,825	1,807	2,141	2,641	2,879	51.8

Source: Central Statistical Office; Labor Force Survey (several). World Bank staff calculations.

The main reason for concern is that the cohort of new labor market entrants is particularly at disadvantage in the labor market. A majority of the unemployed new entrants have only primary and vocational education or less (54 percent), raising further the difficulties they face in entering the currently very competitive labor market (Table 1.4). Indeed, while other factors (e.g., gender and location of residence) contribute in determining employment status, age and educational attainment clearly dominate the odds of an individual being unemployed and long term unemployed.

Table 1.4 Educational Attainment of the Unemployed New Labor Market Entrants, First Quarter 2000

	Thousand	%
Tertiary	32	5%
Post-secondary	16	3%
Vocational Secondary	150	25%
General Secondary	84	14%
Basic Vocational	210	35%
Primary and less	113	19%

Source: Central Statistical Office; Labor Force Survey 1st Quarter 2000
         World Bank staff calculations.

The low levels of educational attainment among this group of new labor market entrants are of particular concern because the shift in labor demand toward more skilled workers has accelerated during the last two years. This is reflected in the fact that less-skilled workers (i.e., those with lower educational attainment) account for almost three-quarters of the unemployed, despite accounting for just over half of the labor force. This shift in labor demand reflects, among other things, screening procedures by employers, who are increasingly relying on educational attainment as a signal of worker's intrinsic abilities. This is especially true for the new jobs being created in the service sector, particularly in the Warsaw area. Most of the high employment growth services such as hotels and restaurants, financial intermediation, real estate and business activities, and public administration disproportionally concentrated in Warsaw, and very high employment growth services such as renting of machinery and equipment, computer services, and R&D are almost entirely confined to the Warsaw area.

The low levels of educational attainment are also a concern because they compound the other problems faced by new labor market entrants in the job market. Payroll taxes are high (39 percent of gross wages), creating a wedge between labor costs and wages that both burdens employers and discourages labor supply, especially when access to social benefits is an available option (Figure 1.4). While workers pension contribution (old age and disability) account for 84 percent of payroll taxes, the other 16 percent of this wedge funds a variety of programs, including training for the unemployed and early retirement programs. Also, the minimum wage in Poland is high relative to the average wage (40 percent), placing less-skilled new entrants in a disadvantaged position. Finally, there are also limitations on fixed-term and by-task employment contracts, which under other circumstances could provide opportunities for new labor market entrants to gain experience. Current legislation, however, limits the cumulative duration of successive fixed-term or by-task contracts. These can only be renewed twice before being automatically transformed into contracts of indefinite duration. The government's concern is that without limitations these labor contracts would become a drain of potential social security contributions. While the issue of social security coverage is understandable, it needs to be weighed against the opportunity cost of having a large share of the youth unemployed, as well as the costs of funding subsidized employment programs for recent school graduates.

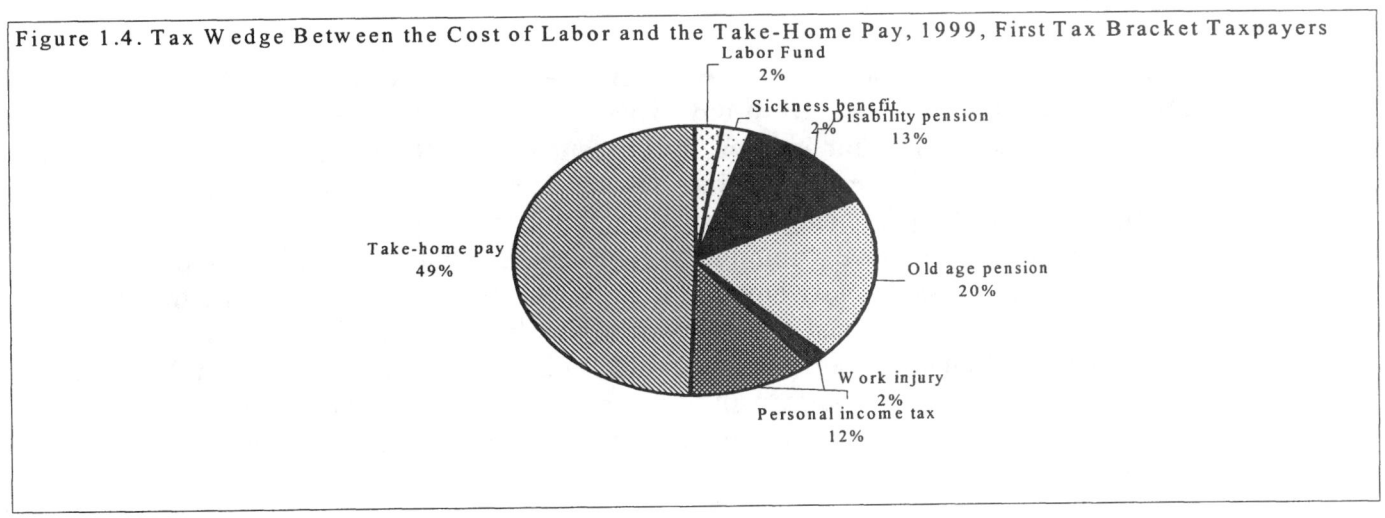

Figure 1.4. Tax Wedge Between the Cost of Labor and the Take-Home Pay, 1999, First Tax Bracket Taxpayers

Source: Ministry of Finance

In summary, the profile of the unemployed that emerges from the recent increase in unemployment is different in three important ways. There is a greater number of displaced workers from the wave of enterprise restructuring that followed the Russia crisis; there is an increase in the number of new labor market entrants; and there are discouraged workers registering as unemployed because unemployment buffers have been exhausted and there are administrative incentives to register. Since the new administrative rules are encouraging individuals to register as unemployed, a lot of the attention has focused on the rising unemployment rate. Concerns should be centered, however, on the underlying labor market trends: (a) the shift in labor demand toward more skilled workers, rendering many workers less employable; (b) barriers in the transition to new jobs, leading many workers toward underemployment and unemployment traps; and (c) the close link between poverty and unemployment, making action to facilitate the transition from old jobs to new jobs even more urgent. Factors contributing to limiting the employability of the current batch of new labor market entrants include low educational attainment. Barriers in the transition to new jobs include the high wedge between labor costs and wages limits on the expansion of fixed-term and by-task labor contracts, and a binding minimum wage for less-skilled workers.[14] Actions to increase the rate of job creation should aim at reducing these barriers and improving workers skills, especially in rural areas.

The rest of this study expands on this account of recent developments, elaborating on four main themes:

- **The recent increase in unemployment results primarily from an acceleration of job reallocation, where jobs being created differ saliently from the job being destroyed, both in terms of skills required from employees and the location of employment.** Chapter 2 draws on the analysis of detailed firm-level data to estimate the rate of job creation and job destruction, examining where are jobs being created and destroyed. It also examines the factors driving the acceleration in job creation and job destruction – the increased integration with the EU and the push toward higher labor productivity, discussing what this implies for future labor market developments.

- **The high rates of unemployment among less-skilled workers reflect several barriers in the transition from old to new jobs, including a binding minimum wage, high taxes on labor income, and incentives for the unemployed to remain in rural areas.** Chapter 3 examines the barriers less-skilled workers face in the transition from the jobs being destroyed to the jobs being created. It looks first at how the minimum wage compresses earnings distribution, limiting employment expansion. It considers next how the high payroll tax and access to state transfers, such as early retirement and unemployment benefits, encourages workers to stay in rural areas and engage in informal activities. Finally, it looks a regional differences in employment and unemployment, discussing how the size of the service sector, education levels and aspects of the labor market legislation constrain job creation in less developed regions of Poland.

- **A policy agenda for job creation needs to include measures to increase flexibility at the lower-end of the wage distribution, initiatives to reduce taxes on labor income, and efforts to improve workers skills, especially in rural areas.** Chapter 4 expands on the empirical analysis of Chapters 2 and 3, elaborating on these policy proposals. It begins by considering options for increasing wage flexibility, ranging from setting a lower minimum wage for new labor market entrants to the regional differentiation of the minimum wage and reducing payroll taxes. It considers next proposals for reforming the labor market legislation, especially measures to reduce

---

[14] Dismissal costs are also high, ranging between 1 and 3 month's remuneration, plus 45 days' notice. In the case of large establishments –with more than 1,000 employees—there are procedural steps aimed at slowing down the dismissal process, increasing these costs to up to 9 months pay.

the compliance costs for small and medium enterprises and efforts to standardize work norms across increasingly disparate working arrangements. It turns finally to measures to improve workers skills and education, including improvements in school curricula, increasing the efficiency of public spending in education, and better targeting training programs.

- **Key for reducing the pool of long term unemployed is reforming labor market programs, minimizing the risks of creating unemployment traps.** Chapter 5 reviews the Polish experience with labor market programs, highlighting how ambiguities in their regulations and misguided incentives (both for participants and program administrators) have contributed toward reducing the effectiveness of the programs. The chapter then examines options for reform that target those in greatest need and encourages participants to return to the job market.

CHAPTER 2. JOB CREATION AND JOB DESTRUCTION

Introduction

The rate of net job creation in Poland over the last decade was very low, averaging less than 1 percent per annum.[15]   It is, therefore, often claimed that the Polish labor market is stagnant, labor mobility is low, and restructuring has been limited. It is also usually argued that this is due to a protective employment legislation and the presence of strong trade unions. These claims are hard to reconcile with the evidence. Poland has sustained a rapid economic expansion for the last eight years, averaging over 5 percent real GDP growth, in the context of intense economic restructuring. Also, Poland's employment protection legislation is among the least strict in the region (Table 2.1), and the strength of the trade unions is felt mostly in the public sector and in state-owned enterprises.

This chapter draws on the analysis of firm survey data to assess the extent and pace of job creation and job destruction in Poland. The analysis shows that the rates of job creation and job destruction have been relatively high in Poland, especially at the initial stage of the transition in early 1990s, and again, after a temporary decline, in the late 1990s. This indicates that the labor market in Poland has been more dynamic and restructuring more advanced than so far has been assumed. These finding support an alternative explanation for the recent increase in unemployment. Unemployment results from an acceleration of job destruction in the context of intense economic restructuring, notwithstanding the continuing increase in job creation. The jobs being created differ however in a salient way from the jobs being destroyed, since jobs are moving from low to higher productivity activities, requiring better skilled workers.

Table 2.1 Summary Indicators of the Strictness of Employment Protection Legislation, late 1990s[1]

	Regular Employment	Temporary Employment	Collective Dismissals	Overall EPL Strictness			
				Version 1[2]	Rank[4]	Version 2[3]	Rank[4]
Czech Republic	2.8	0.5	4.3	1.7	3	2.1	3
Estonia	3.1	0.0	0.0	0.0	5	0.0	5
Hungary	2.1	0.6	3.4	1.4	1	1.7	1
Poland	2.2	1.0	3.9	1.6	2	2.0	2
Slovak Republic	0.0	0.0	0.0	0.0	4	0.0	4
Slovenia[5]	0.0	0.0	0.0	0.0	(4)	0.0	(4)

1) Indicators range from 0 to 4 according to the degree of strictness.
2) Average of indicators for regular contracts and temporary contracts.
3) Weighted average of indicators for regular contracts, temporary contracts, and collective dismissals.
4) All rankings increase with the strictness of employment protection.
5) Based on proposed labor code.
Source: OECD (1999) Employment Outlook, and World Bank staff estimates for Estonia, Slovak Republic and Slovenia.

---

[15] Measured by the census (registration) data, the average rate of net job creation during the 1993 to 2000 period was 0.95 percent, although the census data tends to overestimate employment in agriculture. Measured by the labor force survey, the rate of net job creation during this period was much lower, averaging 0.5 percent.

The rest of the chapter presents the evidence supporting this interpretation of recent labor market developments. It begins by examining measures of job re-allocation, discussing what is driving this reallocation and its links to unemployment. Next, it turns attention to job flows, identifying where jobs are being created and where they are being destroyed. It also discusses the factors driving employment growth – aggregate demand shocks and productivity shocks, conjecturing what this implies for future labor market developments. The chapter closes with a summary of the main conclusions.

Job Reallocation in the Polish Labor Market

As mentioned above, the received wisdom is that the Polish labor market is rather stagnant and characterized by relatively low mobility (Faggio and Konings 1999, Bell 2000, Kwiatkowski et al. 2000). In particular, Faggio and Konings claim that in Poland the job reallocation rate (job turnover), is similar to that in *regulated* labor markets in Western Europe (e.g., Germany) and substantially lower than in *flexible* labor markets such as the UK or the US. Like most other authors, they attribute the apparently low job reallocation rate in Poland to employment protection legislation and the presence of strong trade unions.

An analysis of job turnover in Poland for the years of 1993, 1996 and 1999 indicates that the rates of job creation and job destruction are comparable to other OECD economies (Table 2.2).[16] Poland's average job turnover rate in the 1990s was in the middle of the OECD range, at around 17.5 percent, and among the highest for continuing establishments.[17] The job turnover rate in continuing firms in Poland was around 13 percent in 1999, compared, for example, with less than 10 percent for the UK and the US (in the late 1980s). Obviously, restricting the sample to continuing firms distorts the picture, as for example in the US most of job turnover springs from job openings and closures. Still the point remains valid that job flows in Poland are comparable in magnitude to those observed in developed market economies.

In one important respect, Poland is different from other OECD economies. In Poland, a much larger share of job turnover is accounted for by job destruction than by job creation. Specifically in Poland, job losses account for over 60 percent of the job turnover, while in all other OECD countries under consideration, they account for less than 50 percent.[18] While in Poland job turnover results largely from job destruction, in other countries it predominantly results from job creation. This is a significant difference, which implies that welfare costs of the given rate of job reallocation are higher in Poland than in developed market economies.

---

[16] Gross job turnover is the sum of gross job creation and gross job destruction. The *gross job creation* rate measures the sum of all employment gains in expanding firms in a given year, divided by total employment at the beginning of the year, while the *gross job destruction* rate measures the sum of all employment losses in shrinking firms in a given year divided by total employment. *Employment* is in turn defined as the number full-time wage and salary workers on permanent contracts (i.e., seasonal and temporary workers are excluded).

[17] In the case of Poland data on job turnover in *continuing* firms are more accurate and comparable with other countries than those on job turnover in *all* firms. The reason is that firm closures and associated job losses are significantly under-represented in the Polish data set (which is based on the survey of operating firms) and accordingly job turnover is underestimated.

[18] For the sake of comparability these two figures refer to continuing firms only.

Table 2.2 Job Reallocation[1] – Poland and Selected OECD Countries

	Poland [2] 1993-99 [3]	France 1984-91	Germany 1983-90	Italy 1987-92	United Kingdom 1985-91	United States 1984-91
Gross job gains	8.4	12.7	9.0	11.0	8.7	13.0
Openings	3.4	6.1	2.5	3.8	2.7	8.4
Expansions	5.0	6.6	6.5	7.3	6.0	4.6
Gross job losses	9.1	11.8	7.5	10.0	6.6	10.4
Closures	0.8	5.5	1.9	3.8	3.9	7.3
Contractions	8.3	6.3	5.6	6.2	2.7	3.1
Net employment change	-0.7	0.9	1.5	1.0	2.1	2.6
Job turnover	17.5	22.4	16.5	21.0	15.3	23.4
Continuing establishments only	13.3	12.9	12.1	13.5	8.7	7.7

1) Average annual rates as percent of total employment.
2) Data refer to firms rather than establishments.
3) Average from the three years: 1993, 1996, 1999.
Source: OECD and World Bank staff calculations.

The fact that restructuring is being driven by job destruction does not imply that job destruction in Poland has been consistently high by OECD standards. Poland's indicators were at the bottom end of the OECD range in terms of job creation and in the middle of the range in terms of job destruction during most of the 1990s. The average annual gross job gains accounted for over 8 percent of total employment in Poland, less then in all OECD countries in the sample. At the same time, the average annual gross job losses accounted for 9 percent. The latter is more in Germany and the UK, but less in France, Italy or the US. In 1999, however, Poland witnessed an significant increase in both job creation and job destruction. The former reached the level which is moderate by the OECD standards (10 percent), while the latter reached the level that is relatively high (11 percent). These results portray a dynamic labor market, characterized by relatively intense job reallocation and mobility, notwithstanding the higher rates of job destruction. Also, while the faster pace of job reallocation at the end of the decade was driven by an acceleration of job destruction, there was no slowdown in job creation (Figure 2.1).

Figure 2.1 Gross Job Gains and Job Losses, 1993-99

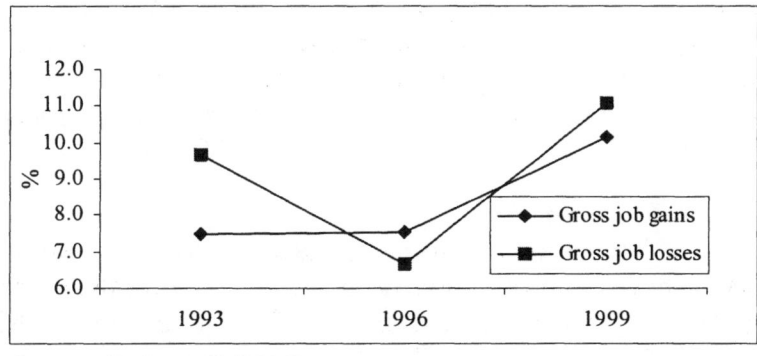

Source: Rutkowski (2001).

Job Flows: Where Are Jobs Created and Where Are They Lost?

Most of the new jobs are being created in the relatively underdeveloped service economy and in industries experiencing rapid productivity growth (Table 2.3). The top 10 industries in job creation include the transport industry; some branches of manufacturing (coke and petroleum products, motor vehicles, rubber and plastic products, publishing); services (insurance and pensions, hotels and restaurants, and other business activities); wholesale trade; and public administration. Among these, transport, coke, petroleum, insurance and pension funds stand out as the largest creators of new jobs, with the number of jobs created by expanding firms accounting for at least 30 percent of initial employment.

The top 10 industries in job destruction include several of the industries and services in the top job creation list. These are transportation, motor vehicles manufacturing and other business activities, indicating that a large share of the job flows happened between firms of the same industry or service (see more below). Other industries where job destruction was high include some branches of manufacturing (basic metals, transport equipment, leather, textiles), coal mining and agriculture. Coal mining stands out as by far the largest declining industry with a 5.6 percent share in employment and an 18 percent job destruction rate.

Table 2.3 Top 10 Industries with Highest Rates of Job Creation and Job Destruction Rates, 1999

Industry	Job creation rate	Share in employment	Industry	Job destruction rate	Share in employment
Land Transport	34.0	2.3	**Land Transport**	23.0	2.3
Coke and refined petroleum products	32.0	0.7	Basic metals manufacturing	22.4	2.2
Insurance and pension funding	30.1	1.1	Transport equipment manufacturing	19.6	1.5
Publishing	20.9	0.6			
Other business activities	19.7	2.4	**Other business activities**	19.4	2.4
Hotels and restaurants	17.3	0.8	Leather products	18.1	0.6
Wholesale trade	15.9	4.6	Coal mining	17.8	5.6
			Textiles	16.9	1.4
Motor vehicles manufacturing	15.0	1.0	Agriculture	16.0	1.1
Public administration and defense	14.9	4.7	Other transport	15.8	3.3
Rubber and plastic products	14.9	0.8	**Motor vehicles manufacturing**	15.1	1.0
Total	x	19.1	Total	X	21.4

Note: The ranking is based on industries whose share in total employment is at least 0.3 percent (1st quartile), meaning that one-fourth of industries with lowest employment were left out of the analysis.
Source: Rutkowski (2001).

Most of job reallocation happens within the same industry. The fact that industries included among those with high job destruction rates are also among those creating most jobs, indicates that a share of job reallocation happens within the same industries. Almost 80 percent of the excess job reallocation are the result of labor moving from declining firms to growing ones within the same industry.[19] This feature of job flows has two very important implications. First, it signals that economic restructuring, as measured by excess job reallocation, does not

---

[19] It is important to note that the predominance of within industry job reallocations is a typical feature across the world, not specific to Poland (see for instance Haltiwanger, 2000).

necessarily imply only job destruction. On the contrary, economic restructuring and job creation often go hand in hand, implying that employment protection may act as a deterrent to job creation. Second, factors leading to job creation act primarily at the firm level, not the industry level, indicating that policies aimed at creating (or saving) jobs at the industry level are missing a fundamental point about the functioning of the labor market. Job creation hinges more on a favorable investment climate at the firm level than on support to a particular industry.

The rest of this section examines three other dimensions of job flows, attempting to answer what accounts for job creation. It looks at job flows within and across regions, at job flows within and between public and private firms, and at differences in job flows by firm size. The findings underscore the robustness of the results reported above. Job creation across regions and within firms are strongly correlated with job destruction, indicating that economic restructuring and employment growth go hand in hand. Most of the job flows happen within regions or within firms in the private sector. Also a surprisingly large share of new jobs comes from start-ups, highlighting the strong link between investment and job creation.

Job flows within and across regions. The rates of job creation and job destruction vary considerably across regions within Poland (Figure 2.2, panels A and B). Job flows range from about 15 percent in Mazowieckie and Wielkopolskie to less than 8 percent in Lodzkie, Slaskie, Dolnoslaskie, and Malopolskie. The most successful regions create twice as many jobs as the least successful ones. Also, job creation and job destruction rates can be very different between neighboring regions with similar degree of urbanization and industrialization. For example, the job creation rate in Mazowieckie (capital region) is twice as high as in neighboring Lodzkie, despite the fact that Lodz is Poland's second largest city. Similarly, the job destruction rate in Opolskie is at the upper end of the distribution, exceeding 16 percent, notwithstanding the fact that Opolskie neighbors have done particularly well in avoiding job destruction (Slaskie), and encouraging job creation (Wroclawskie).

Figure 2.2 Gross Job Creation (A) and Gross Job Destruction (B) by Region, 1999 (%)

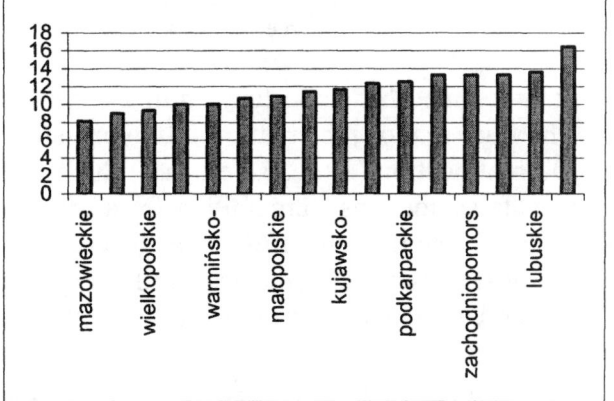

Source: Rutkowski (2001).

The other interesting observation is that most of the job reallocation happens within regions (86 percent), with a smaller fraction (14 percent) happening between regions. The small magnitude of job flows between regions reflects the fact that a vast majority of Polish regions experienced a net fall in employment in 1999 and only a few (4 out of 16) experienced any employment growth. Accordingly, the scope for reallocation of jobs away from declining regions toward growing regions was limited. This result also points to low inter-regional mobility of labor and thus supports an often-held view that Polish regions (voivodships) form separate, relatively independent labor markets.[20]

Public vs. private sector. The job turnover in the private sector is markedly higher than in the public sector, as one would expect (Figure 2.3). The difference lies predominantly in the rate of job creation, rather than in the rate of job destruction. The private sector creates annually over twice as many jobs (relative to its employment) than the public sector. The rates of job destruction are, by contrast, virtually the same in both sectors. This is not surprising if one takes into consideration that the privatization of the Polish economy is an ongoing process, and that a balance between private and public sector employment has not yet been reached. This is expected to continue over the next several years, as privatization allows the private sector to continue expanding, while the public sector contracts.

Figure 2.3 Job Reallocation by Firm Ownership, 1999

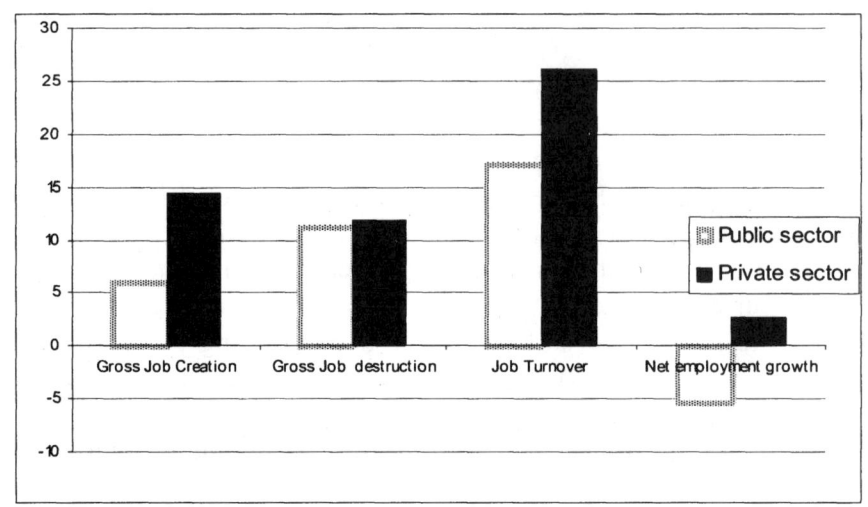

Source: Rutkowski (2001).

The other important finding is that job reallocation is being driven by the private sector. The high rate of job creation in the private sector (over 14 percent) implies a high rate of excess job reallocation (over 23 percent). Such a high rate means that in 1999 almost 12 percent of all private sector jobs were shifted from dying firms to expanding firms. By contrast, in the public sector the comparable figure was 6 percent—half as much as in the private sector. This confirms the observation made in the introductory chapter that industrial restructuring in Poland has been driven largely by job reallocation within the private sector.

Job creation and firm size. The popular view is that small firms create jobs, while large firms destroy them. Is this popular view correct? Only partly correct. Small and micro enterprises have higher rates and job creation than larger firms. The rate of job destruction is relatively uniform across all sizes of enterprises (Table 2.4). However, since larger firms account for a higher share of employment, the popular perception that large and extra-large firms

---

[20] Section IV in Chapter 3 examines the factors accounting for large differences in job creation across regions.

account for most of the jobs lost is correct. Almost 60 percent of total job loses occurred in firms employing more than 200 workers, and as much as 70 percent of job loses took place in firms employing more than 100 workers. The surprising finding is that 46 percent of the new jobs were created by business start ups of varying size.[21] Existing micro-enterprises (1 to 5 employees) account for only 3 percent of the new jobs, while extra-large firms (over 200 employees) were responsible for 16 percent of the jobs created. The role of business start-ups in creating new jobs indicates how improving investment climate and lowering the cost of starting a business, including the costs of creating the first job, can play an important role in generating employment growth.

Table 2.4 Job Turnover by Firm Size, 1999

Firm size	Gross job creation	Gross job destruction	Job turnover	Employment growth	Excess job reallocation	Share in employment (%)
Micro: 1-5 employees	30.0	11.1	41.1	18.9	22.2	1.0
Small: 6-20 employees	10.7	9.0	19.8	1.7	18.1	8.7
Medium: 21-100 employees	7.1	9.8	16.9	-2.7	14.2	26.7
Large: 100-200 employees	5.2	9.8	15.0	-4.7	10.3	12.0
Extra large: 200+ employees	2.9	13.1	16.1	-10.2	5.8	51.6

Source: Rutkowski (2001).

What is Driving Job Reallocation?

The evidence presented up until now indicates that the Polish labor market is undergoing intense restructuring, with jobs being destroyed in low productivity industries and created in high productivity areas. It also indicates that most of this is happening within the same industries and regions, and that the process of job creation is spurred by the entry of new firms. What is driving this reallocation? This has been a subject of intense debate, with some observers indicating that restructuring is driven by aggregate demand shocks resulting from the choice of stabilization and trade policies, while others argue for the importance of productivity shocks that reflect, among other things, progress in privatization.

This section aims at measuring the relative importance of these factors and, in doing so, understand the causality link between them. To understand how these factors are intertwined consider, for instance, the shift in the factor content of Polish exports to the European Union (Figure 2.4). Polish exports moved from being heavily skewed toward unskilled labor-intensive products (textile, garments, furniture, glass, etc.) to a more balanced basket of exports, where skilled labor-intensive products emerge as the fastest growing group (communications equipment, television and radio sets, etc.). More importantly, the growth rate of natural resource intensive exports (food, beverages, raw materials, animal and vegetable oils, leather, plywood, etc.), that depends on labor at the lower-end of the skill level, declined during the 1989-93 period, and stagnated thereafter.[22]

---

[21] Note that the share of job creation by "start-ups" may be biased upward since the coding in the GUS survey does not distinguish between 0s (genuine start-ups) and missing values. Accordingly, some existing firms for which initial employment level was missing might have been mis-categorized as start-ups.

[22] The export specialization index is calculated as the ratio of Polish exports to the EU to the share of total EU external imports.

Figure 2.4 Poland: Export Specialization Index, 1990-98

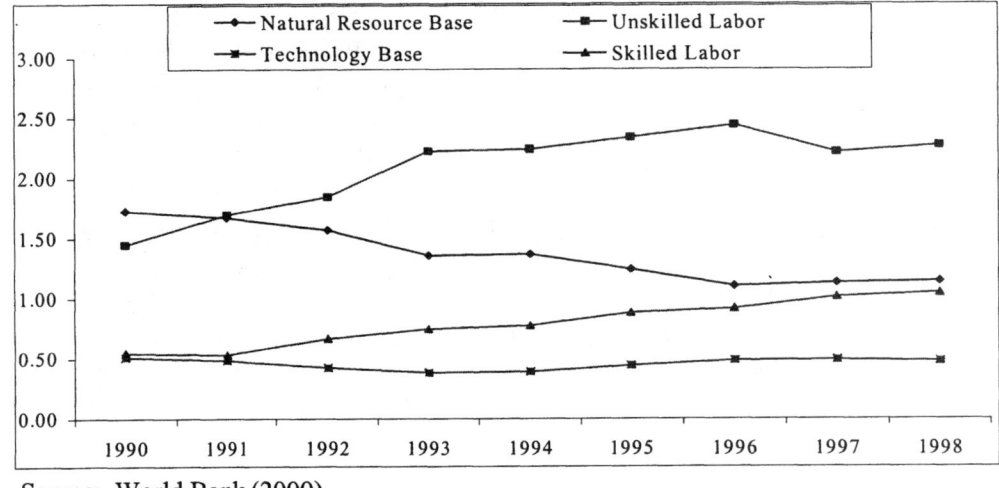

Source: World Bank (2000).

The shift in factor content of Polish exports clearly describes the shift in labor demand toward more skilled workers. This process conceals however a more important, albeit subtle, causality effect running from foreign trade to productivity growth and the sustained expansion of domestic demand. The combined effect of these factors is what is ultimately driving changes in employment. To capture the relative importance of these factors we decompose changes in manufacturing employment into changes in domestic demand (apparent consumption), exports, imports and average labor productivity.

The decomposition is based on the following accounting identity:[23]

$$r_E = r_D(D/Q) + r_X(X/Q) - r_M(M/Q) - r_P$$

where r represents, respectively, the rate of change of employment (E), domestic demand (D), exports (X), imports (M), and productivity (P) – Q represents total output.

The accounting decomposition was applied to 14 manufacturing industries over 1994-98 period, and the results are summarized by the median values for all industries presented in Table 2.5. The results indicate that on average aggregate demand shocks and productivity shocks had offsetting effects during this period. The job creating effect of aggregate demand shocks outweighed productivity shocks in 1996-97, with the opposite happening in 1994 and 1998.

---

[23] A more precise definition is that this formula is based on two accounting identities, where we substitute one identity into the other, differentiate them with respect to time and disregard second order interaction terms. While this approach is a useful tool for the determination of the relative importance of major factors behind changes in employment, there are two shortcomings. One shortcoming is that it assumes fixed input-output co-efficients. This, however, should not be a significant shortcoming over a relatively short time horizon, where one may expect that changes in the production coefficients were much less significant then other factors. Another shortcoming is that this approach lacks any behavioral content, failing to capture possible interdependence between the accounting components. For instance, productivity and demand for goods are related, as gains in productivity tend to raise domestic consumption and exports. Also, increases in imports force firms to act more competitively and rationalize production processes, which results in productivity gains. The decomposition formula will explain a fall in employment by increases in productivity without recognizing that those gains might have been resulted from import competition.

Within the aggregate demand shocks, the job-creating effect of exports were much smaller than the job-displacing impact of growing imports, and both were far outweighed by the labor-generating impact of rising domestic consumption. Instead, the contribution of exports to employment growth resulted primarily from allowing the economy to sustain growth in domestic demand by helping finance part of the growth in imports, which in turn were key for higher productivity growth.

Table 2.5 Decomposition of Employment Change: Median Industry Values for 1994-98 (%)

(% CHANGE)	1995/94	1996/95	1997/96	1998/97	Average
Employment, actual	-0.32	1.65	0.39	-2.02	-0.08
Aggregate Demand	12.36	12.71	14.46	4.28	10.95
Domestic consumption	14.09	15.95	17.43	10.21	14.42
Exports	5.11	2.55	3.41	1.87	3.24
Imports	-6.84	-5.79	-6.38	-7.80	-6.70
Productivity	-11.79	-6.40	-14.20	-8.73	-10.28
SUM	-0.34	1.78	0.43	-2.18	-0.08

Source: Central Statistical Office (GUS) and World Bank staff calculations.

Employment growth and productivity gains. The labor-saving impact of productivity shocks, and the link between productivity and imports is made even clearer by examining the decomposition of employment changes among the several industries within manufacturing (Table 2.6). Large reductions in employment appear to be more common in capital intensive industries (e.g., chemicals, transport equipment, machinery and equipment) making efforts to raise productivity to face the competition from imports.

Table 2.6 Decomposition of Employment Change in 1994-95 (%)

	Employment	Apparent consumption	Exports	Imports	Productivity	Sum
Food, beverages, tobacco	2.24	8.96	0.24	-0.64	-6.18	2.38
Textiles and textile products	1.16	0.97	4.78	-5.15	0.55	1.15
Leather and leather products	-1.53	8.59	5.31	-5.69	-9.88	-1.68
Wood products	2.61	8.76	4.86	-3.62	-7.20	2.80
Pulp, paper, publishing	-1.04	21.65	6.67	-10.69	-18.86	-1.23
Coke, refined petroleum	-0.36	6.40	0.57	-1.37	-5.98	-0.38
Chemicals	-4.21	18.67	8.32	-13.89	-18.07	-4.97
Rubber and plastics	4.56	20.83	5.79	-9.63	-11.90	5.10
Other non-metallic minerals	-0.27	9.33	1.57	-6.11	-5.09	-0.29
Basic metals and fabricated metal products	3.37	18.64	4.36	-7.57	-11.68	3.76
Machinery and equipment	-1.38	31.23	4.92	-15.25	-22.59	-1.69
Electrical and optical machinery	-0.87	30.81	7.41	-18.91	-20.36	-1.05
Transport equipment	-3.20	13.44	6.27	-9.96	-13.37	-3.62
Other manufactured goods	9.46	14.74	12.14	-2.73	-13.42	10.73

Source: Central Statistical Office (GUS). World Bank staff calculations.

While the short-run impact of productivity on employment has been negative, there are good reasons to be optimistic about the long-term effects of productivity growth on employment. Much of the negative impact of productivity on employment in the first decade of transformation reflects that fact that Poland began the transition with excess employment in most State-owned enterprises, since labor hoarding was standard practice under central planning. A large amount of labor shedding was therefore inevitable. Also, looking at aggregate employment by sectors is misleading. While sectors experiencing rapid productivity growth, in particular manufacturing, did not account for a large share of net job creation during the 1990s, they were responsible for a large share of the new jobs being created (Table 2.7). Over the period 1992 to 1998, the net hiring rate, defined as the ratio between net hires over total employment, is positive for the industrial sector, as well as for services, while its negative in agriculture and construction. Finally, rapid productivity growth should lead to higher exports, allowing a sustained expansion in domestic demand and employment.

Table 2.7 Net Hiring Rate, 1992-98 (%)

	1992	1993	1994	1995	1996	1997	1998	Average
Agriculture, hunting and forestry, fishing	-2.4	-1.9	-0.8	-0.5	-0.3	0.0	-0.3	-0.9
Industry	-3.9	3.3	-0.1	0.7	1.5	1.0	-0.7	0.3
Construction	-5.7	-7.3	-3.8	1.0	2.5	4.3	0.7	-1.2
Services	-0.6	-0.3	1.3	1.3	2.1	2.6	2.3	1.2
Total	-2.3	-0.2	0.1	0.6	1.3	1.6	0.8	0.3

Source: Central Statistical Office (GUS). World Bank staff calculations.

While manufacturing is not expected to increase its share of employment much beyond its current levels (20 percent), it will generate demand for employment in the service sector, especially in those sub-sectors in services (renting machinery and equipment, computer services, R&D, and other business activities) that have strong links with manufacturing. Indeed, the future growth in employment will depend, to a large extent, on an increasing integration between services and industry. The growing division of labor among sectors will require a complex network of services such as transport, communications, financial and other business services. This division of labor is expected to increase with time (especially with the deepening in trade integration with the EU), since privatization and increasing economies of scale will lead more businesses to outsource these service activities. Furthermore, the increase in regulations, ranging form standards of quality to the environment, will lead to the emergence of specialized services, such as legal, tax, auditing, and training services.

Realizing this job growth potential will depend, however, on several factors. Chief among them is aligning the skills of the work force to the needs of the emerging service sector. Also important is providing an institutional framework that better suits this new labor market. This includes keeping labor costs in line with labor productivity, formalizing arrangements for fix-time and by-task jobs, and allowing more wage flexibility, especially at the lower-end of the wage scale. The next chapter turns its attention to these issues.

Conclusion

This chapter examined the extent and character of the restructuring of the Polish labor market in the 1990s. The main findings are as follows:

- The Polish labor market has exhibited a large degree of dynamism with relatively high rates of job creation and job destruction by OECD standards. The downside is that most of this dynamism has been driven by a rate of job destruction that exceeded the rate of job creation.

- Most of the new jobs were created in the relatively underdeveloped service economy and in industries experiencing rapid productivity growth. The latter also happened to be some of the top industries in job destruction. This finding indicated that most of the job reallocation happened between firms of the same industry, which has two important policy implications. First, it signals that economic restructuring, as measured by excess job reallocation, does not only imply job destruction. On the contrary, economic restructuring and job creation often go hand in hand, implying that employment protection acts as a deterrent to job creation. Second, factors leading to job creation act primarily at the firm level, not the industry level, indicating that policies aimed at creating (or saving) jobs at the industry level are missing a fundamental point about the functioning of the labor market. Job creation hinges more on a favorable investment climate for individual firms than on support to particular industries.

- Most of the job reallocation happened within the same region (voivodships) (86 percent), with a smaller fraction (14 percent) happening between regions. The small magnitude of job flows between regions reflected the fact that a vast majority of Polish regions experienced a net fall in employment and only a few (4 out of 16) experienced any employment growth. This result indicates that the scope for reallocation of jobs away from declining regions toward growing regions was limited during the 1990s. This result also points to low inter-regional mobility of labor, supporting an often-held view that Polish regions (voivodships) form separate, relatively independent labor markets.

- The job turnover in the private sector was markedly higher than in the public sector. The difference lied predominantly in the rate of job creation, rather than in the rate of job destruction. The private sector created annually over twice as many jobs (relative to its employment) than the public sector. The rates of job destruction were, by contrast, virtually the same in both sectors.

- Small and medium enterprises exhibited higher rates of job creation than larger firms, while the rate of job destruction was relatively uniform across all sizes of enterprises. Almost half of the new jobs were created by business start ups, suggesting that policies to improve the investment climate and to lower the costs of starting businesses, including the costs of creating the first job, should play an important role in a strategy for job creation.

- The job creating effect of increases in aggregate demand was almost completely outweighed by the job saving effect of rising productivity. Within aggregate demand, the job creating effect of exports was much smaller than the job displacing effect of increases in imports, but the net effect was more than compensated by strong growth in domestic consumption. The contribution of exports to job creation resulted primarily from allowing the economy to sustain the growth in domestic demand by helping to finance part of the growth in imports. The latter in turn were key for maintaining high productivity growth, sustaining overall growth.

CHAPTER 3. LABOR MARKET TRANSITIONS

Introduction

The previous chapter indicated that the Polish labor market is quite dynamic, with job creation matching closely job destruction, as it would be expected in a market economy. There is one important difference, however. In Poland the rate of job destruction is currently higher than the rate of job creation, reflecting among other things the fact that many of those who lose their jobs find it difficult to re-enter the labor market. This chapter asks what are the main barriers workers encounter in this transition from old to new jobs. Three main findings emerge:

- *Wages for less-skilled workers are set above market clearing levels*, limiting their employment and encouraging their substitution by better skilled workers earning slightly higher wages. The average difference in wages between workers with basic vocational education and workers with general secondary education is around 13 percent. This relatively low wage premium reflects the impact the minimum wage has on setting a floor on wages for low-skilled workers. Throughout the 1990s, the minimum wage was set at around 40 percent of the average wage and set uniformly at the national level, not accounting for differences in price levels across regions, as well as differences in labor market conditions. This placed less-skilled workers, especially those in less developed regions, at a particular disadvantage. Not surprisingly, workers with basic vocational education or less account for almost three-quarters of all unemployed, with two thirds of them living in rural areas in Poland.

- *Taxes on labor income are high, accounting for 51 percent of gross wages.* This creates a wedge between labor costs and wages that both burdens employers and discourages labor supply, especially when early retirement and access to other social benefits are an option. Some of those who fall into unemployment might find that living on social transfers (social assistance, family benefits, unemployment benefits, etc.) is preferable to working at the minimum wage, losing benefits, and paying taxes. Social transfers are in general lost when individuals accept a job, work longer hours, or take other initiatives to improve income. Calculations of marginal effective tax rate, net of cash transfers, indicate that the increase in net taxes can be as high as 120 percent for individuals moving from unemployment to a job paying the minimum wage.

- *Factors slowing the adjustment in labor supply also affect job creation.* Comparing several factors influencing the hiring rate across the regions within Poland,[24] we found that four factors accounted the most. These are (1) the size of the service sector; (2) the share of the working age population with secondary education or more; (3) the level of labor productivity relative to wages; and (4) the degree of wage flexibility, especially at the lower-end of the wage distribution. The results confirm that higher productivity leads to higher rates of job creation, indicating that

---

[24] These included the economic structure of the regions (e.g., the share of services in total employment, the size of the private non-farm sector) and the availability of infrastructure (e.g., roads, railways, telephone lines).

investments in human capital have a high payoff for both the community and the individual. They also corroborate the notion that limitations on wage adjustments at the lower-end of the wage distribution constrain job creation. More importantly, the results gave support to the notion that, while changing the rules on setting the minimum wage may lead to an increase in wage inequality, it is a price worth paying to avoid an even greater inequality – inequality in the access to jobs.

This chapter documents the importance of these factors. It is organized as follows. It begins by examining how a relatively compressed earnings structure has been particularly disadvantageous for less-skilled workers, delaying adjustments in the labor supply, and encouraging the replacement of less-skilled workers. Next, it considers how high taxes on labor income and access to early retirement, as well as other social transfers, have encouraged displaced workers to exit the formal labor market. In many instances, they have returned to rural areas, seeking self-employment in agriculture and other forms of informal labor contracts. Finally, the chapter examines whether skills and institutional barriers also contribute to the low rate of job creation, especially in less developed regions of Poland. The chapter closes with a summary of the main conclusions.

Skills Mismatch, Compressed Wage Distribution and the Slow Adjustment in Labor Supply

One of the most lasting developments in Polish labor market through the nineties is the shift in labor demand away from less-skilled workers. The shift is best captured by the increase in the share of the labor force with higher (tertiary and post secondary) and medium (general secondary and secondary vocational) education, while there is a decline in the share of workers with basic vocational education or less. As a result, throughout this period workers with basic vocational education or less account for an increasing share of the unemployed and the long-term unemployed (Table 3.1).

Table 3.1 Selected Labor Market Indicators, 1992-99 (%)

	1992	1993	1994	1995	1996	1997	1998	Change 1994-98
Share of the labor force with[1]								
Higher education	...	...	12.8	13.2	13.8	14.0	14.7	14.8
Medium education	...	...	29.2	29.5	29.3	30.4	31.0	6.2
Lower education	...	...	58.0	57.3	56.9	55.6	54.3	-6.4
Share of the unemployed with basic vocational education or less	67.4	69.6	71.3	71.4	71.1	73.3	72.1	7.0[2]

1) Higher education includes tertiary and post-secondary education, medium education includes general and vocational secondary education; lower education includes basic vocational and primary education or less.
2) Changes between 1992 and 1998.
Source: Central Statistical Office; Labor Force Survey (several). World Bank staff calculations.

The importance of education in defining employment status is confirmed by regression results indicating that the level of educational attainment is, after age,[25] the single most important

---

[25] Gender is also an important factor in increasing the odds of being unemployed, as women account for over half of the unemployed. See Box 4.1.

factor increasing the odds of an individual being either unemployed or long term unemployed (Table 3.2).[26] The odds of being unemployed or long term unemployed increases by over 50 percent as an individual's educational attainment falls from general secondary to basic vocational education.

Table 3.2 Odds of Being Unemployed and Long-Term Unemployed by Educational Attainment[a]

	Unemployed	Long-term Unemployed[b]
Post secondary	2.0	2.9
Secondary Vocational	2.4[a]	3.6
General Secondary	2.0	3.7
Basic Vocational	3.7	5.9
Primary or less	3.3	7.2
Number of observations	53,300	52,830

a) Compared to worker with tertiary education. All the estimated coefficients are significant at the 1 percent level.
b) An unemployed person searching for a job for over 12 months is classified as long term unemployed.
Source: Central Statistical Office. Labor Force Survey (several). World Bank staff calculations.

This problem of skills mismatch is reflected even among new labor market entrants that join the unemployment pool. Throughout most of the 1990s new entrants with basic vocational education or less accounted for about two-thirds of those immediately entering the unemployment pool (Table 3.3). More recently, this situation has worsened with marked increase among unemployed new labor market entrants with medium education (general and vocational secondary). While this increase in unemployment among slightly better educated new labor market entrants reflects the overall worsening of labor market conditions, the basic trend is still clear: new entrants from vocational schools (primary and secondary) fare worse in the labor market. This trend is particularly worrisome for new labor market entrants in rural areas, where educational attainment is lower than in urban areas. Indeed, by age 21 about 85 percent of the rural population has dropped out of school, limiting the proportion of post secondary school graduates to less than 15 percent per cohort. Less than 5 percent of the 15 to 21 cohorts in rural areas complete general secondary education, about 20 percent complete secondary vocational education, about 20 percent achieve primary education, 40 percent graduate from basic vocational education.[27] In contrast, in urban areas individuals stay in the school system about three additional years. It is only by age 24 that 85 percent of the cohort has dropped out of school. Furthermore, by age 24 it is apparent that near 30 percent of the cohort will complete post-secondary and higher education. Only about 5 percent of the cohort abandons the school system with primary education; 25 percent with basic vocational education; 10 percent with general secondary education; and 30 percent with secondary vocational education.

---

[26] These findings are based on multivariate logistic regression that investigates the independent impact of a set of explanatory variables on the following categorical variable: whether a person is unemployed or not, and whether a person is long-term unemployed or not.

[27] These figures are for February 1999. They represent the proportion of individuals that is out of the school system –grouped according to their completed schooling—and the proportion of individuals that attends school by age. While this is the result of a cross section of individuals of various ages, it is a good proxy for the pattern of out-of-school transitions for the current 15-21 cohort.

Table 3.3 Distribution of Unemployed New Labor Market Entrants by Educational Attainment, 1992-2000 (%)

	Nov-92	May-93	May-94	May-95	May-96	May-97	May-98	Feb-99	Mar-00
Higher education	**6.2**	**5.2**	**4.4**	**3.0**	**3.9**	**4.0**	**5.3**	**7.9**	**8.0**
Tertiary	3.3	1.7	1.6	1.6	1.2	1.0	2.3	4.4	5.0
Post-secondary	2.9	3.5	2.8	1.4	2.7	3.0	3.1	3.5	3.0
Medium education	**25.9**	**26.1**	**28.1**	**31.6**	**30.3**	**27.6**	**30.0**	**30.0**	**39.0**
Vocational Secondary	7.9	18.0	19.6	22.2	20.4	18.2	17.3	21.1	25.0
General Secondary	18.1	8.2	8.5	9.3	9.9	9.4	12.6	8.8	14.0
Lower education	**67.9**	**68.6**	**67.5**	**65.4**	**65.8**	**68.4**	**64.7**	**62.2**	**54.0**
Basic Vocational	47.4	42.6	41.0	40.2	43.9	42.7	41.0	36.3	35.0
Primary and less	20.4	26.0	26.6	25.3	21.9	25.7	23.7	25.8	19.0

Source: Central Statistical Office. Labor Force Survey (several). World Bank staff calculations.

What other reason could explain the fact that labor supply has been slow to adjust to changes in skill requirements? One factor that could be contributing to the slow adjustment in labor supply is that the differences between the demand for and the supply of less-skilled workers has not translated into an equivalent widening in earnings differentials (Table 3.4).[28] The earnings of those in the bottom 10 percent of the distribution still account for around 56 percent of the median earning, down from around 60 percent at the beginning of the decade. Most of the increase in inequality is attributable to the increase in earnings of those on the top ten percent of the distribution. Also, most of the increase in wage difference between these two groups happened in the first half of the decade (1992-96), and has remained relatively stable since then.

Table 3.4 Earnings Distribution, 1992 - 1998

	1992	1993	1994	1995	1996	1997	1998	1999	Change 1992-99 (%)
Earnings relative to the median:									
Bottom 10%	61.6	60.1	57.6	58.1	56.9	56.6	57.1	56.1	-8.9
Top 10%	179.8	181.9	195.0	197.3	199.5	200.3	194.1	199.7	11.1
Decile Ratio[a]	2.92	3.03	3.39	3.40	3.50	3.54	3.40	3.56	22.0
Earnings inequality (Gini*100)	24.7	26.0	28.1	28.8	29.5	30.1	29.3	...	18.6[b]
Incidence of									
Low Pay[c] (%)	14.2	15.7	17.2	17.3	18.3	18.8	18.2	18.7	31.7
High Pay[d] (%)	7.0	7.2	9.5	9.6	9.8	10.0	9.1	9.8	40.0

a) Top decile over bottom decile.
b) 1992-98.
c) Less than 2/3 median.
d) More than 2 median.
Source: Central Statistical Office, Earnings Survey (several). World Bank staff calculations.

[28] Another factor that might be contributing to the slow adjustment in labor supply is the international migration of young workers. While permanent migration has declined considerably since the beginning of the 1990s, temporary migration continues to be very significant. A micro-census in 1995 showed that about 900,000 Polish citizens spent more than 2 months abroad. This figure may well include persons who may not actually return to Poland. Since there is no information available from Polish statistics, we can assume that a large proportion of these temporary migrants travels to Western Europe on official work visas. Information available from German statistics shows that in the mid-1990s approximately 150,000 persons from Poland entered Germany as seasonal laborers to work mostly in agriculture, hotels and restaurants. A smaller number entered as contract workers employed mostly in the construction sector. It is likely that an additional number of temporary migrants worked abroad without a working visa.

This asymmetry in the adjustment of relative wages is confirmed by looking at the change in relative wages across occupational categories. Most of the adjustment happened in the relative wages of workers at the upper end of the skill distribution. White-collar workers share an across the board increase in relative wages, with occupations at the very top of the skill ladder experiencing the highest increase. The relative wages of legislators, higher officials and managers experienced an increase by 13 percent, rising from 60 percent to 80 percent over the average wage between 1992 and 1998. Professionals saw their relative wages increase from 16 percent to 24 percent over the average wage, and clerks experience rise from 89 percent to 94 percent of the average wage. The increase in earning inequality is comparatively smaller among blue-collar workers, with workers with elementary occupations seeing little change at all. Workers in agriculture and fishery, craft workers and plant and machine operators record declines ranging from 2 percent to 4 percent, which is comparatively smaller than the increase among workers at the higher end of the skill distribution (Table 3.5).

Table 3.5 Relative Wages by Occupation, 1994-1998

	1994	1995	1996	1997	1998	Change 1994-1998 (%)
Legislators, senior officials and managers	1.59	1.59	1.64	1.67	1.81	13.7
Professionals	1.16	1.16	1.21	1.25	1.23	6.7
Technicians and associate professionals	1.07	1.09	1.09	1.09	1.09	2.2
Clerks	0.89	0.91	0.92	0.92	0.94	5.8
Service workers	0.78	0.78	0.76	0.76	0.76	-2.3
Skilled agriculture and fishery workers	0.82	0.83	0.81	0.80	0.79	-3.4
Craft workers	0.98	0.98	0.97	0.96	0.94	-4.0
Plant and machine operators and assemblers	1.03	1.03	0.98	1.00	1.00	-3.6
Elementary occupations	0.72	0.75	0.71	0.71	0.73	0.5

Source: Central Statistical Office; Labor Force Survey (several).

What accounts for this asymmetry in earnings adjustment? The two main factors slowing the adjustment in earnings at the lower-end of the skill distribution are the floor that the minimum wage imposes on earnings, and the stronger bargaining power of workers in State Owned Enterprises (SOEs), where there is a large representation of low-skilled blue collar workers. Throughout the 1990s, the minimum wage was set at around 40 percent of the average wage, clearly compressing the lower-end of the wage distribution -- and this compression was higher in the State sector (Table 3.6). Although many workers in state-owned enterprises do not actually earn the minimum wage,[29] the minimum wage serves as a floor for wage negotiations,[30] making them an important constituency supporting a relatively high minimum wage.

---

[29] Indeed, the private sector reports greater incidence of low pay than the State sector, with private sector workers earning on average 18 percent less. The low average wage in the private sector, compared to the public sector, may, however, reflect underreporting by the private sector for tax reasons, as well as a focus on money wages rather than on fringe benefits.

[30] While State sector wages are in principle defined by the tripartite committee composed by representatives of the government, employer's association and trade unions, in practice wage increases have consistently exceeded the levels defined in the committee's guidelines.

Table 3.6 Minimum Wage Ratios, 1991-99

	1991	1992	1993	1994	1995	1996	1997	1998	1999
Minimum Wage Ratios									
Minimum Wage/ Average Wage in the State Sector (%)	41.0	47.3	46.7	45.8	46.5	45.9	45.0	43.0	40.8
Minimum Wage/ Average Wage in the Private Sector (%)	35.6	42.4	42.3	42.9	42.5	41.8	40.9	39.6	38.3

Source: Central Statistical Office; Earnings Survey (several). World Bank staff calculations.

A review of the data available from 1998 earnings survey indicates that workers in State Owned enterprises (SOEs) enjoy wages significantly higher than their counterparts in the private sector. On average, wages in SOEs are almost 40 percent higher than in private domestic firms, although similar to wages in foreign owned enterprises. This premium exist irrespective of the size of the enterprise, although the premium is higher in small (50 employees) and very large (over 1,000 employees). The reason is that small and very large enterprises, both in the public and the private sector, place greater reliance on less-skilled workers and, as the examples above illustrate, the public sector tends to pay workers in this skill category slightly higher wages.

What accounts for this public sector wage premium? The likely source of this wage premium is the strong bargaining power of trade unions in the public sector, while their representation in the private sector is weak -- if any at all. This public sector wage premium has two negative effects on employment. It comes at the expense of firms profits, implying that SOEs invest less than they would have if they paid competitive wages. Lower investment, in turn, implies lower labor productivity and lower job creation. Also, wages above market clearing levels cause unemployment, as more workers desire to work at a given wage than firms are willing to employ them.

How can SOEs afford to pay higher wages? Some SOEs still face a soft budget constraint. The best example is the mining industry, that is both directly subsidized by the state budget and relies on indirect subsides in the form of non-payments of taxes and social security contributions. Unsurprisingly, the incidence of minimum wage earners is the lowest among SOEs, 0.6 percent, compared to 8.5 percent in private domestic firms and 1.8 percent in private foreign firms. The compression was higher in State sector, in part because of the presence of State-owned enterprises with a large representation of low-skilled blue-collar workers.

Is there evidence of substitution of workers with lower educational attainment for workers with higher educational attainment? The wage premium for workers with secondary education relative to workers with basic vocational education is around 13 percent, which is low considering that the productivity resulting from a few more years of education probably exceeds this average wage difference. This has probably acted as an incentive to substitute away from workers with less education, especially in the emerging service sector. For instances, during the 1994-98 period there was a 13 percent increase in the number of employees with secondary education, while workers with basic vocational education or less saw no increase at all in employment. When comparing across broad economic sectors, the rate of substitution was highest in those sectors making new hires (e.g., public and private services) and in sectors experiencing increases in labor productivity, such as utilities and manufacturing. Only those sectors experiencing secular declines, such as mining and quarrying, saw an increase in the share of workers with basic vocational education or less, probably reflecting the departure of workers with better job opportunities outside the mining sector (Table 3.7).

Table 3.7 The Ratio between Workers with Secondary Education and Workers with Basic Vocational Education or Less Employed in Selected Economic Sectors, 1994/1998

	1994	1995	1996	1997	1998	% change
Total	50.3	51.4	51.6	54.6	57.2	13.7
Mining and quarrying	44.3	40.2	45.3	41.5	41.1	-7.2
Manufacturing	47.5	45.8	44.5	47.7	49.4	4.0
Electricity, gas and water supply	70.5	64.7	70.5	69.1	82.2	16.6
Construction	40.9	39.8	34.5	31.0	35.3	-13.7
Services[1]	95.3	96.8	95.8	105.1	104.6	9.8
Public services[2]	126.8	133.3	138.5	137.7	144.9	14.3

1) Services include trade and repair, hotels and restaurants, transport, financial intermediation, real estate and business activities.
2) Public services include public administration and defense, education, health and social work, other community, social and personal services.
Source: Central Statistical Office Labor Force Survey (several). World Bank staff calculations.

In summary, wage rigidities at the lower-end of the wage distribution are one of the factors accounting for higher than average unemployment rates among less-skilled workers. Chief among these rigidities is the bargaining power of trade unions in State-Owned Enterprises (SOEs). On average, wages in SOEs are almost 40 percent higher than in private domestic firms, although similar to wages in foreign-owned enterprises. Also contributing to the wage compression is the relatively high minimum wage, set at around 40 percent of the average wage. The compressed wage distribution has both limited the demand for less-skilled workers and, in some instances, encouraged their substitution for workers with higher educational attainment earning slightly higher wages. This compression is higher in regions where state-owned enterprises are large employers, and in regions with high unemployment.

A compressed wage distribution is, however, only one of the factors slowing the adjustment in labor supply. Other limitations include a high payroll tax and the access to alternative sources of income, such as early retirement and other social benefits. In an environment where the option of early retirement and continuous reliance of social benefits are available, one can observe a shift toward informal labor contracts, especially in rural areas. The next section turns therefore to these other barriers in the transition from old to new jobs.

Taxes on Labor Income, Access to Social Transfers and Informal Labor Contracts

This section examines the barriers in labor market transitions that lead workers facing difficulties in the labor market to fall into underemployment and unemployment traps. This includes situations where high taxes on labor income and limitations imposed on the renewal of labor contracts, combined with relatively easy access to early retirement and other social transfers, lead unemployed workers to settle for self employment and part time jobs in low productivity activities. Understanding how these barriers operate, especially for less-skilled workers, is important because policymakers are always caught between providing income support to unemployed workers and finding sources of funding for these programs. Since most programs are funded through payroll taxes, this creates a vicious circle whereby programs designed to assist in labor market transitions also act as a deterrent for the creation of jobs for these same low-skilled workers.

To what extent have workers had to settle for self-employment or part time jobs? The extent to which workers have had to settle for less than full time, regular jobs is captured in the February 1999 snap shot of the distribution of employment by status (Table 3.8). There is an increasing reliance on alternative forms of labor contracts, particularly in sectors that account for most of the growth in employment over the last several years. For instance, 30 percent of the jobs in services provided by the private sector (e.g., trade and repair) are either self-employment or part time. Also, most of the employment in agriculture is either self-employment or unpaid, reflecting the growth of private individual farms, as well as a considerable amount of hidden unemployment in this sector.

Table 3.8 Distribution of Employment by Status, February 1999 (%)

Sectors	Self employment	Full time employment	Part time employment	Unpaid employment	Share in total Employment
Agriculture and fishing	70.9	8.8	1.0	19.3	27.4
Mining and quarrying	0.0	99.6	0.4	0.0	1.9
Manufacturing	6.7	88.0	4.7	0.7	19.5
Electricity, gas and water supply	0.3	97.7	2.0	0.0	1.6
Construction	18.9	76.8	3.9	0.5	5.9
Private Sector Services	22.8	68.8	7.0	1.4	51.2
Trade and repair	29.1	61.4	7.3	2.3	30.2
Hotels and restaurants	22.3	65.4	10.5	1.8	3.2
Transport	17.4	79.5	2.7	0.3	12.3
Financial intermediation	10.4	84.8	4.7	0.0	4.7
Real estate and business activities	15.2	70.4	13.9	0.5	10.8
Public Services	3.8	89.0	7.2	0.0	38.8
Public administration and defense	0.3	96.1	3.6	0.0	6.2
Education	1.0	90.0	9.0	0.0	13.0
Health	2.8	92.0	5.1	0.1	14.6
Other community and social services	15.7	71.6	12.5	0.1	5.0
Total	24.4	66.1	4.9	4.6	100.0

Source: Central Statistical Agency; Labor Force Survey (February 1999). World Bank staff calculations.

The reliance in alternative forms of employment contract is not a novelty in Poland. Private or temporary labor contracts were already part of the Polish reality under central planning in the eighties, when a large legal private non-agricultural sector was allowed to compete with the State sector for labor resources.[31] The key change has been that these activities became more important in terms of employment and their contribution to workers income. For some workers, this has implied greater flexibility in working hours. For others, this has entailed lower pay, and

---

[31] These activities, better characterized as fixed-term or task-driven employment contracts included "praca zlecona," in the case of specifics services that can be contracted out; "pracownik sezonowy," in the case of peak season tasks in agriculture; and "umowa-zlecenie" or "umowa o dzielo", in the case of consultant-type activities among professionals.

greater job insecurity. For many others, however, it has meant settling for self-employment or part time jobs in low productivity activities (e.g., farming).

A survey carried out by the Central Statistical Office in 1998 indicated that some of the high employment growth sectors (trade and repair, hotels and restaurants, transportation, and construction) were, after agriculture, the sectors with the highest degree in informal labor contracts. According to the respondents, their decision to work without registration reflected the absence of formal jobs; the need to avoid social security contributions; and the desire to increase their income. In addition, 10 percent of the respondents said that they decided to work unregistered not to loose their rights to other sources of income, namely pensions and social benefits.

In many cases these motivations for engaging in informal contracts are self-reinforcing. Consider for instance the incentives faced by someone who loses her job, finds it difficult to find a new one, and begins relying on unemployment benefits and other social transfers for survival. This person might find that living on these social transfers (social assistance, family benefits, unemployment benefits, etc.) is preferable to working at the minimum wage, losing benefits, and paying taxes. Social transfers are in general lost when individuals accept a job, work longer hours, or take other initiatives to improve income. Calculations of marginal effective tax rate, net of cash transfers, indicate that the increase in net taxes can be as high as 120 percent for individuals moving from unemployment to low paying job. [32]

Not surprisingly, this practice of collecting pension benefits and other social transfers while still working is especially prevalent in rural areas. During the week of the February 1999 Labor Force survey 14 percent of old-age pensioners, 19 percent of disability pensioners, and 6 percent of unemployment benefit recipients reported having worked in rural areas. They report working as self-employed, part-time, or unpaid workers, since the transfers listed above are incompatible with formal work. It follows that, at least in rural areas, the full time work category corresponds roughly to the 'formal' sector, and the rest are in the 'informal' sector. By this definition, therefore, about half of the workers in rural areas (or 20 percent of all workers, roughly 3 million individuals) are in the 'informal' sector.

Several other factors conspire to keep labor contracts in the farm sector informal. Chief among them is the Farmers' Security Fund (KRUS), which was established in 1990 to provide pensions and insurance in case of accidents or sickness for farm workers. Eligibility to KRUS is dependent on owning at least 1 hectare of land, and contributions are around one-sixth of the contributions to the regular Social Security Fund (ZUS). In principle, as soon as a worker gets a formal job he/she has to start making contributions to ZUS. However, monthly contributions to ZUS amount to approximately one-half of the net wage (20 percent of gross wages), a significantly higher contribution than the one required for KRUS. This significant difference in

---

[32] The following example illustrates this point. Consider the case of an individual that in September 2001 could chose between receiving the unemployment benefit equivalent to PLN 445, or work earning the PLN 770, which was slightly more than the minimum wage at the time, at a low paying job. In this latter case, however, she/he would be paying 51 percent of the gross labor income in taxes (income and payroll). The net income associated with the unemployment benefit would be the same PLN 445, while the net income from working at this low paying job would be only PLN 377, implying a marginal tax rate of 120 percent.

contributions, especially considering that the two systems offer similar benefits, is equivalent to a tax on the movement of workers out of farm employment.

Recent measures adopted by Parliament to curtail the eligibility to pre-retirement benefits and allowances are likely to have similar effects. Pre-retirement benefits and allowances are provided to unemployed workers with a long working record,[33,34] so they can withdraw from the labor market before qualifying for old age pension benefits. The program, which was introduced in 1997, saw a significant increase in applications last year, with the number of beneficiaries exceeding the budget forecast by 62 percent. To limit expenditures under these programs, only unemployed workers in high unemployment areas, who meet the eligibility criteria and do not combine these benefits with other sources of employment income, can now apply. While this does reach the immediate objective of reducing expenditure under this program, the longer term, more corrosive effect, is to encourage individuals to stay in high unemployment areas and engage in informal labor market arrangements to complement their income.

In summary, the combination of high payroll taxes and the access to early retirement and other social transfers acts to create unemployment traps, especially in rural areas. This happens because in some instances the unemployed might find that living on social transfers (social assistance, family benefits, unemployment benefits, etc.) is preferable to working at the minimum wage, losing benefits, and paying taxes. This in turn calls for action to reduce taxes on labor income, as well as measures to prevent that government programs create a disincentive for workers to move away from high unemployment areas. These recommendations are developed in the next two chapters, dealing with policies for job creation, and reforms in labor market programs.

To better understand how factors limiting labor mobility and constraining employment creation exacerbate regional inequalities in job creation, we turn next to a quantitative assessment of the factors influencing job creation at the regional level. While the results confirm that hiring is higher in regions that are urbanized, with high levels of human capital and modern – service oriented – employment structures, they also point to the fact that hiring rates are higher in regions characterized by low unit labor costs, which includes high productivity relative to wages, and a more flexible wage structure at the lower-end of the skill distribution. The latter confirms what was observed from comparing the earnings distribution across regions within Poland, namely that the minimum wage is binding in high unemployment areas.

Do Regional Inequalities Reflect Labor Market Rigidities?

One of the most visible barriers in the transition from old to new jobs has been the large differences in job creation across regions within Poland. Since the beginning of the economic transformation there has been a decline in employment in those regions where previously there

---

[33] Working record requirements are 30 years in case of women and 35 for men, although under certain circumstances the required age may be reduced to 25 and 30 years respectively. Exceptions are also made for individuals with at least 15 years of service in the profession considered as special in the Law on Disability and Old Age Pensions.

[34] The list of special jobs includes among others soldiers, teachers, artists and civil servants. Additionally, people who were employed in difficult and dangerous conditions are also considered as special cases and have reduced pre-retirement benefit age requirement.

was limited output diversification (e.g., regions dominated by large state farms, and in localities that depended on one large industrial employer). There has also been slow growth in employment in regions where the service sector was underdeveloped. The regions most seriously affected are the northern regions that were dominated by State farming, and industrial enclaves such as textile and closing in Lodz, automobile assembly in Starachowice and coal mining in Walbrzych.

The regional disparities in unemployment that emerged in the early 1990s have proven to be remarkably persistent (Table 3.9). Regions where unemployment was high in 1993 still had high unemployment in 2000 despite several years of sustained economic growth, and a gradual overall decline in unemployment. This results from most of the decline in unemployment happening in regions where unemployment was already relatively low, widening the dispersion in unemployment rates between regions (voivodships). For instance, in 1993, the highest regional unemployment rate was 4 times higher than the lowest, with Slupskie at 28.4 percent, compared to Warszawskie at 5.4 percent. By 1998, the last year before the administrative reform, this ratio had increased to almost 8 times, with Slupskie at 20.5 percent and Warszawskie at 2.6 percent. This situation did not change significantly after the 1999 administrative reform that defined new boundaries for the regions (voivodships). The only noteworthy change was a marked reduction in unemployment differences across regions as a result of higher unemployment rates at the lower-end of the distribution. While this reflects an overall increase in unemployment during this period, it also results from the fact that larger regional units imply smaller differences in unemployment rates between them.

Table 3.9 Regional Unemployment (%)[1]

	1991	1992	1993	1994	1995	1997	1998	1999	2000
Maximum	18.6	26.6	30.3	29.8	28.4	21.2	20.5	21.4	24.5
Minimum	4.2	6.4	7.6	6.5	5.4	2.7	2.6	8.7	11.1
Max/Min	4.4	4.2	4.0	4.6	5.3	7.9	7.9	2.5	2.2

1) The January 1999 administrative reform changed the boundaries of the regions.
Source: Central Statistical Office, Annual Statistical Yearbook (several). World Bank staff calculations.

This relative stability of regional differences in unemployment rates reflects very low internal migration flows. In 1998, for instance, the official statistics report a total net outflow from rural areas of 8,500 persons at working age, which, even under the assumption of high under-registration of migration, is negligible compared to the 2.3 million people unemployed at the time. While there was a link between unemployment and migration, the link was weak with only extreme levels of unemployment generating significant responses in terms of migration.[35]

The explanations for this low level of migration range from a poorly functioning housing market to observations that migrant face a much higher probability of being unemployed.[36] This

---

[35] A regression analysis of the factors driving migration indicates that unemployment is a significant factor explaining migration, although the relationship is weak. This finding is consistent with an examination of the data, since a positive net inflow migration is registered only in those regions (voivodships) with the lowest unemployment rates: Mazowieckie (Warszawa), Wielkopolskie (Poznan), Malopolskie (Krakow), Slaskie (Katowice) and Pomorskie (Gdansk). All the other regions (voivodships) experienced a net outflows.

[36] This finding is reported in Chlon (1998), who uses micro data to estimate the differences in the probability of being unemployed between migrants and non-migrants.

is not surprising since the overwhelming majority of migrants (80 percent) have only basic vocational education or less, and most are less than 34 years old (Figure 3.1). Their decision to migrate, despite the higher odds of remaining unemployed, likely reflects the fact that they are not eligible to many of the incentives to stay in rural areas described in the previous section. Indeed, the importance of these incentives in encouraging older workers to either stay or return to rural areas is clearly reflected in the data, where most of the outflow from urban areas is by individuals in the 35 to 64 age bracket (Figure 3.1).

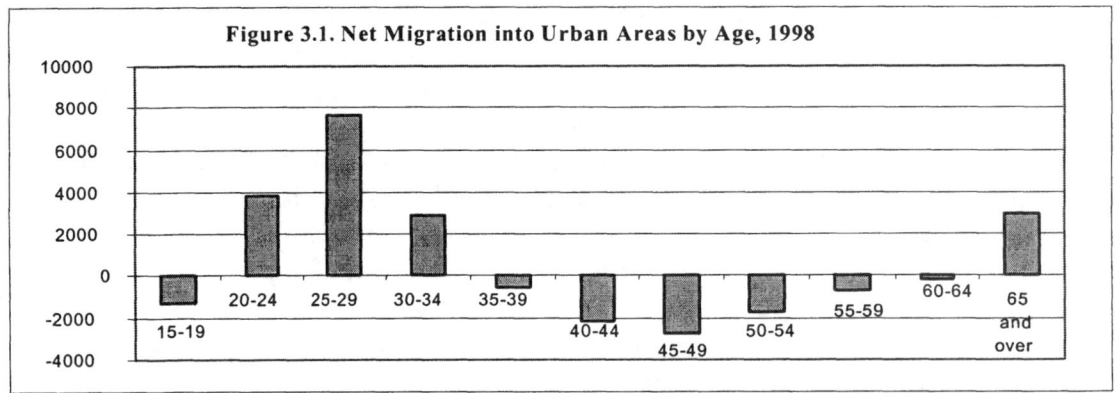

Source: Central Statistical Office.

Have skills and institutional factors constrained job creation? In the absence of large internal migration flows,[37] regional units provide a useful reference to measure the main structural determinants of job creation. The regions are all subject to the same policies at the national level, and have specific endowments that influence the rate of job creation. Comparing their performance allows us to understand which policies are binding, and which endowments make a difference. This is especially important when employment services are being further devolved to the regions, and additional funds (including forthcoming funds from the EU) will be made available for regional development.

To understand what are these structural determinants of job creation at the regional level, we regress the hiring rate on several structural factors for each region.[38] These included:

- the economic structure of the region (e.g., the share of the services in total employment, the size of the private non-farm sector);

- indicators of capital stock and labor productivity (e.g., capital labor ratio, labor productivity per worker);

- indicators of human capital (e.g., the share of the population with less than secondary education);

---

[37] Although there is a significant amount of commuting and a process of suburbanization, with most of the urban growth happening in town with populations in the 50,000 to 100,000 range.

[38] The hiring rate was used as a proxy for job creation because statistically it showed the strongest correlation with key variables of local labor market conditions. The hiring rate is associated with net hiring rate, which is an indicator of new job creation, and the availability of vacancies. It is also negatively correlated with long-term unemployment and positively correlated with net migrations to the region.

- indicators on the labor market structure (e.g., wage level, labor costs per unit, and the ratio between the top and the lowest 10 percent of the wage earns); and

- indicators of the availability of infrastructure (e.g., road, railways, telephone lines).

We found that four factors account for most of the regional differences in job creation:

- The economic structure of the region, where regions with a developed service sector hire much more workers than regions where the service sectors is less important.

- The human capital of the region, since the hiring rate is higher the larger the proportion of the population with secondary or higher education.

- The level and structure of wages, since the hiring rate is significantly higher in regions where productivity is high relative to wages.

- The wage dispersion in the region, which is an indication of wage flexibility at the lower-end of the earnings distribution.

Together, these four factors explained 83 percent of variance in hiring rates across regions. Other factors were largely unimportant, including factors such as the quality of infrastructure in the region. The strongest factors determining differences in the hiring rate were education and the employment structure. A one standard deviation increase in the share of population with secondary or higher education led to a 0.45 standard deviation increase in the hiring rate, everything else held equal. A similar effect on the hiring rate would occur with the one standard deviation increase in the share of services in employment.

The hiring rate was also sensitive to changes in wages and unit labor costs. If the level of wages in a region were to rise by 1 percent then we might expect the hiring rate to fall by 0.9 percent (productivity and other variables held constant). This implies that an increase in the wage level, if not matched by a proportional increase in productivity, is likely to result in lower hiring.

Finally, the hiring rate is influenced by wage dispersion. A more compressed wage distribution, especially at the bottom, results in lower hiring. For instance, a 10 percent increase in wages at the bottom decile of the wage distribution (increase relative to the median wage) would lead to a 12.7 percent decrease in the predicted hiring rate.[39] Alternatively, a 10 percent decline in wages at the bottom decile of the wage distribution would lead to an 8.5 percent increase in the predicted hiring rate. This result confirms that raising the minimum wage is likely to negatively affect the hiring of less-skilled workers, especially in less-developed regions.

In summary, a region's broadly defined economic structure and the flexibility of the labor market were key factors influencing the availability of job opportunities. Hiring was higher in regions that were urbanized, with high levels of human capital and modern – service oriented – employment structures. Hiring was also higher in regions characterized by low labor costs,

---

[39] A 10 percent increase in the ratio of the bottom 10 percent of the wage distribution, relative to the median, would occur if wages of the bottom decile earners rose by 10 percent, while the median wage remained constant.

which included high productivity relative to wages, and a more flexible wage structure at the lower-end of the skill distribution.

Conclusion

This chapter examined barriers to transitions from old to new jobs within the Polish labor market. These include wage rigidities, especially at the lower-end of the skill distribution; taxes on labor income; and lower rates of job creation in regions outside the Warsaw metropolitan area. Three main findings emerge:

- *Wages for less-skilled workers are set above market clearing levels*, limiting their employment and encouraging their substitution for better skilled workers earning slightly higher wages. The average difference in wages between workers with basic vocational education and workers with general secondary education is around 13 percent. This relatively low wage premium reflects the impact the minimum wage has on setting a floor on wages for low-skilled workers. Throughout the 1990s, the minimum wage was set at around 40 percent of the average wage and set uniformly at the national level, not accounting for differences in price levels across regions, as well as differences in labor market conditions. This placed younger, less-skilled workers, especially those in less developed regions, at a particular disadvantage. Not surprisingly, workers with basic vocational education or less account for almost three-quarters of all unemployed, with two thirds of them living in rural areas in Poland.

- *Taxes on labor income are high, accounting for 51 percent of gross wages.* This creates a wedge between labor costs and wages that both burdens employers and discourages labor supply, especially when early retirement and access to other social benefits are an option. Some of those who fall into unemployment might find that living on social transfers (social assistance, family benefits, unemployment benefits, etc.) is preferable to working at the minimum wage, losing benefits, and paying taxes. Social transfers are in general lost when individuals accept a job, work longer hours, or take other initiatives to improve income. Calculations of marginal effective tax rate, net of cash transfers, indicate that the increase in net taxes can be as high as 120 percent for individuals moving from unemployment to a low paying job.

- *Factors slowing the adjustment in labor supply also affect job creation.* Comparing several factors influencing the hiring rate across the regions within Poland,[40] we found that four factors accounted the most. These are (i) the size of the service sector; (ii) the share of the working age population with secondary education or more; (iii) the level of labor productivity relative to wages; and (iv) the degree of wage flexibility, especially at the lower-end of the wage distribution. The results confirm that higher productivity leads to higher rates of job creation, indicating that investments in human capital have a high payoff for both the community and the individual. They also corroborate the notion that limitations on wage adjustments at the lower-end of the wage distribution constrain job creation. More importantly, the

---

[40] These included the economic structure of the regions (e.g., the share of services in total employment, the size of the private non-farm sector) and the availability of infrastructure (e.g., roads, railways, telephone lines).

results gave support to the notion that, while changing the rules on setting the minimum wage may lead to an increase in wage inequality, it is a price worth paying to avoid an even greater inequality – inequality in the access to jobs.

The challenge for Polish policymakers is to increase efforts to improve workers skills, especially in rural areas, and to provide for a labor market institutional framework that better accommodates the demands of the new economy. This includes reducing taxes on labor income, reducing limitations on fixed term and by task contracts, and most importantly, setting the minimum wage at a level that is not as binding for less-skilled workers. This will require in turn efforts to ensure that worker's basic rights are protected in an environment where worker's representation in the private sector is not as strong as it is in the State sector. In the private sector, wage bargaining is very decentralized, and lifetime employment is the exception rather than the rule. Meeting this challenge is important because expansion in employment will be concentrated in the private sector, where more flexible forms of labor contract are more commonly found. We turn next therefore to policies aimed at reaching this balance.

CHAPTER 4. POLICIES FOR JOB CREATION

Introduction

The findings of the previous chapters indicated that job creation has been closely associated with job destruction, as the continuous economic restructuring has required workers to move from declining to growing firms. While some workers have fared well in this transition from old to new jobs, others have experienced greater job insecurity and lower pay, sometimes having to settle for early retirement or informal jobs in low productivity activities. This results in part from the new jobs created being saliently different from the jobs being destroyed in terms of skill requirements and location. In addition, there are instances where the labor market legislation is binding for the employment of less-skilled workers, especially in the less developed regions within Poland. This is particularly the case of the minimum wage, although the high taxes on labor income and constraints imposed on temporary contracts also limit employment creation for these workers.

These findings have important implications for policymakers, who are constantly balancing demands for increasing job creation and protecting the interests of those currently employed. If job destruction is, however, an inevitable consequence of economic restructuring, emphasis needs to be placed on creating new jobs and assisting temporarily displaced workers, rather than protecting existing jobs. Creating new jobs, especially for less-skilled workers, will require, in turn, efforts to reduce some of the more binding constraints of the labor market legislation, while still ensuring that workers basic rights are protected. It also requires appropriate investment in education and training, so that workers are equipped to compete in today's labor market.

This chapter is organized as follows. It begins by considering measures to increase wage flexibility and reduce taxes on labor income. Next, it examines proposals for reforming the labor market legislation recently presented to the Polish Parliament. Finally, it discusses options for reforming education and training. The chapter closes with a summary of the main conclusions.

Increasing Wage Flexibility and Reducing Labor Costs

A significant share of the attention of policymakers has focused on increasing wage flexibility by changing the rules governing the setting of the minimum wage. This reflects the empirical evidence supporting the notion that the minimum wage in Poland is binding for the employment of new entrants and less-skilled workers, especially in regions outside Warsaw. In their strategy for employment creation and human resource development presented to Parliament in January 2000, the Polish authorities proposed indexing the minimum wage to inflation rather than to average wages, and introducing a separate, lower minimum wage (below the current uniform minimum wage) for the labor market entrants. This would aim at providing some downward flexibility in the minimum wage, especially at a time when large inflows of first-time job seekers are entering the market.

The Government's strategy did little to generate political support. The trade unions resisted changes in the rules setting the minimum wage on the grounds that lowering the minimum wage for new entrants would encourage the replacement of many already employed by younger workers, not leading to a net increase in employment. Estimates of the incidence of minimum wage employment indicate, however, that this argument is not supported by the evidence. The chances of having a low-paid job are by far the highest among young workers with short job tenure. Among young workers (25 years old or less) the incidence of minimum wage employment is 11 percent, against 3 percent among the prime age workers. Similarly, the incidence of minimum wage employment is 10 percent among workers with job tenure of up to 5 years, against 5 percent among workers with tenure of 6-10 years and 2 percent among workers with tenure exceeding 10 years. This indicates that minimum wage employment is characteristic of young, inexperienced workers. The incidence of minimum wage employment among prime-age, more experienced workers is much lower.

The evidence also indicates that the minimum wage is particularly binding for less-skilled workers in less developed regions within Poland. In some of the most depressed regions of the country, such as Slupskie, Wloclawskie and Ciechanowskie, the national minimum wage accounts for well over 90 percent of the median wage for workers in the lower 20 percent of the wage distribution. In Slupskie, for instance, workers in the lowest 20 percent of the wage distribution earn on average only 3 percent more than the national minimum wage, indicating that many low-skilled workers in Slupskie could have been employed if there were a regional differentiation of the minimum wage. Thus, while the differentiation of the minimum wage might lead to an increase in wage inequality, it is a price worth paying to avoid an even greater inequality – inequality in the access to jobs.

The two options faced by the Polish authorities are either setting a lower minimum wage for new entrants, or introducing some regional differentiation of the minimum wage. The case for a lower minimum for new labor markets entrants is based on the evidence presented above that the incidence of minimum wage earning is higher among young, inexperienced workers. A age-differentiation of the minimum wage is also easier to implement and monitor, since the regional differentiation of the minimum wage requires drawing a clear line between the regions within Poland. The case for the regional differentiation of the minimum wage is based on the fact that a minimum wage set at a uniform national level of around 40 percent of the average wage compresses the earnings distribution in less developed regions, hindering job creation in these regions. Setting regional standards for the minimum wage would mitigate this problem. Whatever option the Polish authorities chose to take, there is the need to building a broad consensus around the proposal, not least because changing the rules for setting a national minimum wage would require a constitutional amendment.

What is the employment impact of a lower minimum wage? Estimates presented in the previous chapter indicate that a 10 percent decline in the minimum wage would increase the hiring rate by as much as 8.5 percent. Since price differences between Warsaw and less developed regions are well over the suggested 10 percent decline in the minimum wage, this reduction could be achieved without reducing the minimum wage in regions outside Warsaw below the real minimum wage in Warsaw. Once the regional differentiation is in place, the value of the minimum wage could be preserved by indexing these wages to regional price indices, maintaining their original purchasing parity.

Reforming wage settlement procedures. The reform of the minimum wage could also trigger a broader reform of the wage settlement procedures since the minimum wage has been used to set a floor for industry-wide wage bargaining. The effective impact of this floor is magnified because the minimum wage is linked to the average wage. Wage settlements will need to either be de-linked from the minimum wage because industries in different regions would be subject to different minimum wages, or become employer specific rather than industry-wide agreements.

There are several arguments for moving away from industry-wide wage settlements. Chief among them is the fact that private employers are less likely to engage in industry-wide agreements that do not reflect the particularities of each of the firms involved. This greatly reduces workers bargaining power. In the past, trade unions were able to reach industry-wide agreements because state-owned enterprises could follow uniform employment and wage rules, even if sometimes this implied a few enterprises within the industry had to receive financial support from the state.[41] Today's dominance of private sector employers precludes this option.

If private enterprises do not follow industry-wide agreements, workers will be subject to much less protection. A decentralize wage settlement procedure would provide an alternative to current procedures, allowing workers more protection. To the arguments already presented in favor of decentralized wage agreements, one might add the evidence presented in the second chapter indicating that most job flows happen within firms of the same industry. Industry-wide wage agreements would only reduce the scope for agreement at those firms under greater pressure to reduce employment, accelerating job destruction.

Reducing taxes on labor income. Actions to achieve greater wage flexibility needs to be complemented by efforts to reduce the single most important non-wage labor cost in Poland, the taxes on labor income. This includes the personal income tax and payroll taxes. It is generally agreed that the marginal labor tax wedge may affect both labor supply and demand.[42] In Poland, the average tax rate for a single income earner (personal income tax plus payroll taxes) is 51 percent, and the marginal rate can reach as high as 120 percent for someone moving from unemployment to a low-paying job. In a situation where pre-retirement benefits are an available option, early retirement is widespread, and other social benefits are relatively generous, this high tax wedge is apparently contributing toward reducing labor supply by encouraging eligible workers to withdraw from the labor market. Also, this wedge between labor costs and wages is likely discouraging labor demand, further contribution to the slow expansion of formal employment in the economy.

While steps to reduce the tax wedge on labor have been taken by re-organizing the pension system, aligning benefits and contributions more closely, and by tightening the rules on sickness allowances, more still needs to be done. Options to reduce the tax on labor income include increasing the flat income tax deduction on the personal income tax for low-income

---

[41] Usually in the form of arrears on tax obligations and social contributions, to meet these agreements.

[42] The labor marginal tax wedge is the increase in payments of income taxes and social security contributions associated with an increase in gross labor earnings (gross wage plus employer's contribution to social security).

families with one working adult.[43] Options to reduce the payroll tax will depend, however, on actions on several fronts. This includes (i) curbing the abuse of early retirement, disability and sickness benefits; (ii) identifying alternative sources of funding for active labor market programs;[44] and (iii) eliminating the quota-levy system designed originally to encourage the employment of workers with disabilities.

Poland has taken steps recently to reduce the abuse of early retirement, disability, and sickness benefits. For instance, the extension of sick leaves must now be approved by physicians officially certified by the Social Insurance Office, and the creation of a central register of medical certificates will allow immediate verification sickness claims. The greatest scope for reducing the payroll tax is, therefore, in identifying alternative sources of funding for active labor market programs, and in eliminating the quota-levy system designed originally to encourage the employment of disabled workers. Funding for active labor market programs should be shifted to general taxation, reducing competition between active and passive labor market policies and, with that, concerns that spending on active programs plunge when unemployment is rising. Passive labor market programs could continue to be funded through payroll taxes, albeit at a slightly lower tax rate.

The elimination of the quota-levy system should proceed for two reasons. First, the quota-levy system implies a payroll tax on the workers of firms that chose not to meet the quota of 6 percent of workers with disability. This payroll tax is higher the lower the wage of the individual worker, penalizing the employment of less-skilled workers. For instance, while the levy is set at 2.4 percent, it adds to 6 percent for a regular worker earning the minimum wage because the levy is based on the country's average wage rather than the individual worker's wage or the firm's average wage.[45] Second, while most firms chose to pay the levy rather than hire workers with disabilities, adding the levy to the payroll costs of regular workers, those firms that meet the quota hire workers with slight disabilities – workers that in many countries would not be considered disabled -- failing to accomplish the objectives of the law. Eliminating the quota-levy system would reduce this is additional payroll tax on regular workers, allowing the Polish authorities to consider other options to mainstream workers with disabilities into the workforce. In doing this, Poland would be following the example of other European countries that have recently moved away or reformed their quota-levy system for workers with disabilities.[46]

What would be the impact of lowering payroll taxes on job creation? At present, payroll taxes in Poland and other Central and Eastern European countries are high, even by the standards of other OECD countries (Figure 4.1). This suggests that a reduction in payroll taxes

---

[43] These changes are, in turn, contingent on reducing the tax expenditure programs that today benefit mostly high-income earners. At present, these tax expenditure programs narrow the tax base, limiting the options for unilateral income tax reductions. See Cavalcanti and Li (2000).

[44] This is discussed in more detail in the next chapter.

[45] This follows because the minimum wage is equivalent to 40 percent of the average wage, so 2.4 percent/0.4 = 6 percent.

[46] The UK abandoned their quota system and the Netherlands gave up a planned system. Portugal also considered but decided against the quota system. Ireland and Belgium limited their system to the public sector, while Germany and France have reformed existing quota systems.

would have a significant impact on employment. Assuming a wage elasticity of labor demand of - 0.5, which is at the lower bound for other OECD countries (Table 4.1), a 10 percent reduction in payroll taxes would reduce gross wages by around 4 percent and induce about a 2 percent increase in formal employment.[47]

Figure 4.1. Payroll Tax Rates in Selected OECD and Central and Eastern European Countries (%)

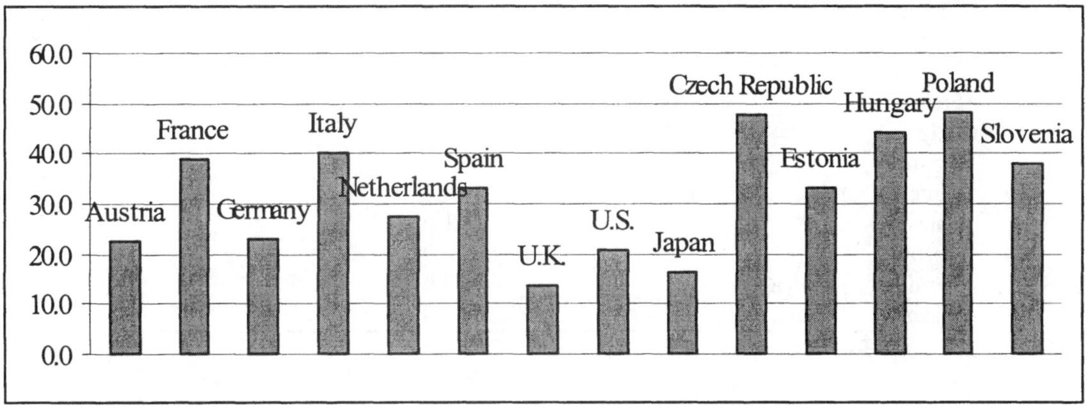

Source: OECD (1999).

Lowering payroll taxes will also have a fiscal impact. Assuming a wage elasticity of – 0.5, the 10 percent reduction in payroll taxes would lead to an 8 percent decline in revenues. While this could be partially offset by a reduction in claimants to unemployment benefits and an by an increase in payroll tax payment compliance due to lower tax rates, these are likely to be relatively minor effects. A reduction in payroll taxes would require therefore either identifying new revenue sources for programs currently funded by payroll taxes, or clearly defining expenditure cuts. Options includes those already listed above: (i) curbing the abuse of early retirement, disability and sickness benefits; (ii) identifying alternative sources of funding for active labor market programs;[48] and (iii) eliminating the quota-levy system designed originally to encourage the employment of workers with disabilities.

Measures to increase wage flexibility and reduce labor costs are only one step toward facilitating job creation, albeit an important step. A related set of issues refers to the modernization of the Polish labor code to reflect changes in the workplace as employment increasingly shifts to the service sector. The next section focuses therefore on recent proposals for reforming the labor code. Most proposals aim at reducing the compliance costs for small and medium enterprises, and at standardizing work norms across increasingly disparate working arrangements. While the immediate impact on job creation is not as clearly measurable as those discussed above, they are an important step in facilitating the transition from lifetime, full-time

---

[47] While this example only captures a partial impact of lowering payroll taxes on employment, it serves the purpose of illustrating the impact of reducing payroll taxes. There are several other factors at play that cannot fit neatly into the example, however. For instance, the example does not consider the issue of tax incidence. If the full burden of the payroll tax does not fall on the payroll, the projected growth in employment will be lower. Also, there is always a time lag between reducing payroll tax rates and the actual increase in employment. This time lag varies significantly depending on labor market circumstances, reaching in some OECD countries as much as seven years (see Table 4.1).

[48] This is discussed in more detail in the next chapter.

employment in industrial settings to flextime employment in the service sector, without compromising worker's basic rights.

**Table 4.1 Wage Elasticities and Employment Responses,
Selected OECD Countries**

Country	Wage Elasticity	Medium Lag (years)
United States	-0.5	3.0
Japan	-1.0	1.0
Germany	-0.8	3.0
France	-1.0	2.0
Italy	-1.0	2.0
Japan	-0.5	5.0
United Kingdom	-1.0	4.0
Canada	-0.5	1.0
Australia	-1.0	2.0
Sweden	-0.9	7.0
Finland	-1.0	3.0

Source: OECD Job Study, 1994.

Reforming the Labor Code[49]

There is an increase perception within Poland that the labor code has become binding for sustaining stronger employment growth. This is especially true in the case of less-skilled workers. While it is sometimes difficult to distinguish between the political rhetoric seen in the press and hard evidence confirming this perception, the analysis presented in the previous chapters does indicate that in some instances the minimum wage is binding for new labor market entrants and less-skilled workers. Also, there is an increase reliance on self-employment and part time jobs in the emerging service sector, suggesting that the high payroll tax and restrictions imposed on temporary contracts are a barrier for the expansion of formal employment. Finally, we have seen that small and medium enterprises play an important role in job creation. This justifies reducing some of the most burdensome aspects of the labor legislation for these firms, especially since the cost of compliance with the labor legislation had larger firms in mind.

This section examines the five most important recent proposals for reforming the Polish labor market legislation, indicating where they stand in reaching a balance between modernizing Poland's labor relations without compromising worker's basic rights, including access to social security. These proposals include revisions of labor market legislation concerning temporary contracts, substitute employees, employment in firms with less than 50 employees and payment for overtime work. In most instances, revisions are designed to bring legislation up to date with modern practices. There is one instance, however, where the proposed revision opens scope for abuse and should be reconsidered to avoid this risk. This is the case of the provision allowing the voluntary suspension of binding aspects of the labor code during periods when the employer is in financial distress.

---

[49] The Polish Labor Code dates from the early 1970s and is geared towards full-time and life-time employment mainly in large State-controlled industrial enterprises and in State-provided services of all kinds. It envisions a major role, at least formally, for trade unions at all levels, and for active State intervention through the Labor Inspectorate.

Temporary contracts. One of the main issues in the current labor code is the limitation on the successive renewal of temporary contracts. At present temporary contracts cannot be renewed more than twice before being automatically transformed in contracts of indefinite duration. This aims at avoiding the risk that firms would meet their personnel needs through successive temporary contracts, abusing their relationship with employees and draining social security of a potential source of income.

The proposals currently in Parliament call for lifting this limitation, claiming that it only encourages hiring without registration especially in the emerging service sector. A revision of this provision of the labor code can be achieved, however, by making the text of the labor code more precise, satisfying the need for more flexibility without opening the door for abuse. For instance, firms and workers could be allowed to enter into subsequent employment contracts for a fixed period. These temporary contracts would have the same legal effect as employment contracts for an indefinite period, provided that no more than a certain number (e.g., three) definite period contracts take place with intervals between contracts of less than one month.

Substitute employees. The Polish labor legislation has no provision for substitute employees. This creates problems for employers that need to find temporary replacement for workers on leave, such as maternity leave. Indeed, there appears to be resistance on the part of employers to hiring women at child bearing age because of the absence of provisions for substitute employees (Box 4.1). There are legitimate reasons therefore for changes to be made to the legislation allowing employers to hire substitute employees due to an excused absence from work. These substitute workers would be issued fixed-term or definite period contracts for the period of the excused absence of the employee from work. These contracts would include competitive wages and the provision of social security benefits as required by laws and regulations. These contracts would be called substitution labor contracts and not be subject to notice of termination.

Box 4.1 What Explains the High Unemployment Rate among Young Women?

While women stay longer in school than men in either urban or rural areas, they still account for a disproportionate share of the unemployed and the long-term unemployed. This is especially true in the case of young women at the ages of 18 to 34. Women account for over 50 percent of the unemployed in this age group, despite the fact that over 30 percent of them have post-secondary, vocational secondary, or general secondary education. Their unemployment rate is not higher because many chose to withdraw from the labor force. Their withdraw from the labor force results, among other things, from the fact that women face greater difficulties than men in finding jobs. A survey of unemployed individuals revealed that only 25 percent of women found work within a year of becoming unemployed, compared to 40 percent of men. The main explanation for this gender difference was marital status, reflecting women's greater responsibility for childcare. This hinders job search and limits employment options. There may also be some discrimination by employers because the labor legislation confers maternity rights to women at childbearing age that employers seek to avoid by simply not employing them. While this legislation reflects the interest of the Polish society in protecting mothers and young children, the burden is being disproportionally carried by those that the legislation aims at protecting.

Source: Cavalcanti (2000).

Employment contracts for firms with less than 50 employees. There is an increasing perception that the compliance costs of the labor code is higher for small and medium enterprises. One example are the provisions in the labor codes requiring any employer employing at least 5 employees not covered by a collective labor agreement to establish the conditions of remuneration for work in remuneration by-laws. Since remuneration by-laws are costly and bureaucratic, there is a proposal currently in Parliament raising the threshold number of employees to 50. While this reduces the compliance costs for many firms, it still leaves open whether there should be clear norms applicable to all enterprises on minimum remuneration standards. This includes basic salaries, bonuses, meal vouchers, and commissions. These forms of remuneration should all be taxable, avoiding the risk that employers combine minimum wages and other means of compensation to not pay payroll taxes and social security contributions.

Standards of remuneration for overtime work. The standards of remuneration for overtime work has been subject to intense debate in Poland. Employers would like to reduce the additional payment required for overtime work from the current levels of 50 percent in the first two hours and 100 percent for any subsequent hours at night, Sundays and other days of rest, to 25 percent and 50 percent respectively. Trade unions see this as a concealed attempt to avoid hiring more workers. There is a legitimate issue on the employer side, however, especially as employment in the service sector becomes more important. A compromise solution would be to standardize the payment for overtime work at 50 percent over the payment for regular hours, and limit overtime to a maximum of 4 hours a day. This is the standard in most OECD countries.

Suspension of binding provisions of the labor code. One of the most controversial proposals for reforming the Polish labor code concerns firms facing a situation of loss of financial liquidity lasting for a period of at least 6 consecutive months and carrying the threat of bankruptcy or liquidation of the employer. The proposal allows the employer to, upon consultation with the trade unions, suspend some of the most binding provisions of the labor code for a period of up to 6 months. This suspension would not apply provisions related to work safety and hygiene, protection of work of juveniles and women, the minimum remuneration for work, the number of work-free days, and the maximum daily and weekly length of working time. These exceptions still leave the door open to considerable amount of abuse, especially in those provisions related to hiring and firing, benefits, and the rules governing collective bargaining. The proposal should, therefore, be reconsidered.

These proposals are sample of the reforms being considered. While many of the proposed changes are unique to Poland, others reflect trends in other parts of the world, especially in countries that are experiencing the transition from industrial to service-based employment. The issues facing countries more advanced in this transition extend beyond those considered above. They include performance-based earnings, part-time jobs, non-premise work, flexible working schedules, telecommuting, and weekend work. As Poland moves further into this transition, workers, employers and policymakers should expect to confront similar issues.

Compliance. Chief among those issues Poland will need to confront is compliance with the exiting legislation, since trading partners, especially trade unions within the EU, will also demand a "harmonization" of how workers are treated. Consider, for instance, the compliance with the existing legislation on health and safety at the workplace. While the Polish legislation on this topic is consistent with EU directives, data available indicates significant underreporting of work-related accidents. In 1999 there were reported around 99,000 work-related accidents in Poland, which is equivalent to about 0.9 percent of employment. This is low by EU standards. For example, the same ratio is 3.5 percent in France (1990), 6.8 percent in Portugal (1989), and 8.1 percent in Spain (1995). This level of reporting is also in contrast with other information from the Polish authorities indicating that in most firms the conditions of occupational health and safety are unsatisfactory, with around 15.7 percent of the Polish labor force employed in adverse or harmful conditions, routinely exceeding the norms for chemicals, dust, and noise.

Improving health and safety conditions will require expenditures by both firms and the State. Assessing the required expenditure is however very difficult, not least because they should be balanced against losses caused by work-related accidents and illnesses, (e.g., loss of output, costs of medical treatment, and administrative costs of public bodies). Estimates of the latter range from 1 percent to 4 percent of GDP (OECD, 1990). Given its worse starting conditions vis-à-vis the EU, Poland's investment in reducing health and safety hazards at work should yield very high returns.[50]

The returns to increasing compliance with the labor market legislation highlights the high returns for both individuals and firms in investing in improving health and safety conditions in the workplace. This should make compliance with labor market legislation an integral element of a job creation strategy for Poland. It should also highlight the importance of other investments in human capital. This is where the study turns next -- to the options to improve workers education and training.

Investing in Workers Education and Training

Measures to facilitate labor transitions within the labor market will have little effect if those entering or re-entering the labor market don't have adequate skills. This in turn requires attention from policymakers to issues of workers education and training. While the Polish labor force is highly educated, comparable to other lower income EU countries, 40 to 45 percent of Poles perform only at the lowest proficiency level of the literacy scales—reading, writing, and quantitative skills. This is in part a result of the fact that over one-half of workers has received basic vocational training or less, which provides skills which are narrow and inflexible. This is also in part due to low levels of participation in continuing education and training courses. It is estimated that only 8 to 10 percent of all employees, and 7 percent of the unemployed, participate in training programs. While employers sent some 41 percent of participants to training, most went mainly for short compulsory industrial safety training courses.

To reverse these trends the government has been taking action in two fronts. It has defined a comprehensive reform of the public and professional education school system, aimed at improving the overall qualification levels and better aligning curricula's with the demands of the labor market. It has also identified a range of measures to encourage greater participation in

---

[50] Another issue that needs to be addressed is the current ambiguity concerning which institution is responsible for enforcement of health and workplace safety laws. The State Labor Inspectorate, directly responsible to Parliament, is charged with monitoring the implementation of collective agreements and health and safety laws, while the Ministry of Labor and Social Protection is responsible for setting standards and enforcing the law.

continuing education and training programs through tax incentives and subsidized loans. The reform of the education system includes a new structure for primary schools and gymnasiums, as well as new options for secondary schools -- specialized lyceums, new vocational schools, a two-year supplementary secondary school. This structural change will be complemented by a new curricula based on qualification standards and a module structure for vocational schools. The measures to encourage participation in continuing education programs include (i) refining existing tax incentives for employers to provide training (e.g., apprentice programs) and for workers to upgrade qualifications; (ii) subsidized loans for individuals to finance education and training costs; (iii) providing training programs for workers in declining industries through voivod labor offices and NGOs (e.g., coal sector, metallurgy, defense); and (iv) greater emphasis on monitoring and evaluation to continually assess the implementation of these programs.

The proposals place emphasis on many of the right issues, and success will depend largely on appropriate implementation. Three issues stand out in implementation: (i) adequate sequencing, so that the assessment of learning achievements can provide timely feedback for allocation of resources and the development of the new school curricula; (ii) rational decentralization of the education system, allowing economies of scale to be fully exploited; and (iii) better targeting of training programs, either provided through the labor offices, or funded through tax incentives. The following paragraphs examine each one of these issues.

Reforming the educational content of school programs. About two-thirds of secondary enrollments are in overly specialized programs of vocational education. Graduates of vocational education programs have one of the highest unemployment rates (over 40 percent) among groups within the labor force. The emphasis of these new curricula should be on skills that are broader, transferable, and in demand. Education should foster creativity and lifelong learning. Some changes along these lines have occurred. Heavy focus on technical education is giving way to a more balanced mix, with social sciences playing a larger role. The curricula and teaching methods are, however, being revised slowly. For example, courses of foreign languages, social sciences and business skills are expanding, but still fall short of demand. The Ministry of National Education should intensify efforts to accelerate change and to reallocate resources to those areas of education for which there is more demand (e.g., out of vocational education and into universal education).

Rather than relying only on changing the curriculum to influence educational programs, the Ministry of National Education should proceed with plans to introduce the national assessment of learning achievement. This is an instrument that can help guide the reallocation of resources by providing an objective measure of student performance, facilitating quality control, and indicating geographical areas and educational programs that require additional funding. Implementation will be very important, especially since this national assessment needs to be implemented promptly. This in turn will require building the needed capacity to design and carry out the testing, as well as the capacity both at the central and the local level to analyze and act upon the results of these assessments.

Action is already being taken toward reaching these objectives. A new secondary school certificate program, reflecting this standardization seeks to harmonize examination requirements and evaluation criteria. The new secondary school final examination will include internal and external written exams in examination centers. This includes two levels of secondary school final examinations: a first level examination covering basic knowledge and skills, and a second level examination required from students planning to enroll in advanced studies. To implement this proposed standardized national learning assessment, a Central Examination Commission and eight regional commissions have been created. The commissions have already defined standard requirements for examinations, analyzing the results and submitting annual achievement reports to the Ministry of National Education (MNE). In addition, these commissions will (i) prepare and disseminate teacher programs on evaluation and examination; (ii) maintain a registry of examiners; and (iii) carry out studies on evaluation and examination. The national assessment system reflects a shift in the evaluation process from focusing on student screening and selection to becoming an instrument for guiding the management of the education system, including curricula development and allocation of resources. The next step is to strengthen the feedback of this process for teachers and students, since examinations conducted at the end of each education level will serve as selection and entrance exams.

Improving the efficiency in the delivery of education services – decentralization and beyond. The decentralization of the education system entails leaving primary schools and gymnasiums with the gmina level (municipal), and transferring secondary and vocational schools to the powiat (county) level. The goals is to achieve efficiency gains by improving accountability and increasing the responsiveness to specific local needs and/or demand shifts. Other elements of the education program should, however, continue to be managed centrally to fully exploit economies of scale. This includes the national assessment discussed above, the development of national curricula, as well as the training and supervisory functions. Actions in other fronts may also improve the efficiency of the education system. In primary and secondary education, for example, greater efficiency can be achieved by increasing student-to-teacher ratios from the current figures of 16 and 18, respectively, to EU standards of 20 to 25. Also, fast-spreading private schools may provide a solution for those that can pay. This should be part of a general move toward financing schemes that include cost-recovery features, such as setting tuition fees for university education, while providing scholarships and student loans to lower income students.

Box 4.2 Does Investment in Education and Training Payoff?

The short answer is yes, and the payoff is highest for the individual making the investment. Two human capital factors explain most of the difference in wages across workers: educational attainment and work experience. Education has by far the most significant and positive effect on the level of earnings, explaining 42 percent of the difference in wages across workers. On average, individuals with university education earn almost twice as much (97 percent) as a person with primary education. The premium on secondary vocational education is a bit lower, but still significant. A worker with secondary vocational education earns on average 32 percent more than a worker with primary education. Work experience also counts, explaining another 33 percent of the difference in wages across individuals. One year of job experience adds, on average, 2.5 percent to an individual's wage.

Source: Cavalcanti (2000).

Targeting training programs. While skills mismatch explains some of the increase in structural unemployment, the experience from OECD countries with training programs for the unemployed is mixed. Broadly targeted training programs seldom raise either employment chances or earnings. Programs targeting particular problems (e.g., for skills in short supply) obtain better results; and the impact is greatest for individuals whose problems are clearly identified and only moderately severe. Better targeting of training programs means focusing training programs on younger adult men and women (25 to 34 years), rather than on older adults and youth. This can be achieved through counseling in the labor offices and better targeting limited public sector resources. One way of better targeting limited public sector resources is containing the abuse of tax incentives by higher income tax payers. Tax incentives that allow deduction of personal income tax payments for expenses on education and training benefit disproportionally higher income tax payers, failing to achieve the intent of policymakers.

Conclusion

This chapter builds on the findings of Chapters 2 and 3 of this study to define a policy agenda for job creation. There are four main proposals:

- *Introduce either age or a regional differentiation of the minimum wage.* The two options faced by the Polish authorities are either setting a lower minimum wage for new entrants, or introducing some regional differentiation of the minimum wage. The case for a lower minimum for new labor markets entrants is based on the evidence that the incidence of minimum wage earning is higher among young, inexperienced workers. An age-differentiation of the minimum wage is also easier to implement and monitor, since the regional differentiation of the minimum wage requires drawing a clear line between the regions within Poland. The case for the regional differentiation of the minimum wage is based on the fact that a minimum wage set at a uniform national level of around 40 percent of the average wage compresses the earnings distribution in less developed regions, hindering job creation in these regions. Setting regional standards for the minimum wage would mitigate this problem. Whatever option the Polish authorities chose to take, there is the need to building a broad consensus around the proposal, not least because changing the rules for setting a national minimum wage would require a constitutional amendment.

- *Reduce taxes on labor income.* Actions to achieve greater wage flexibility needs to be complemented by efforts to reduce the single most important non-wage labor cost in Poland, taxes on labor income. In Poland, the average tax rate for a single income earner (personal income tax plus social contributions) is 51 percent, and the marginal rate can reach as high as 120 percent for someone moving from unemployment to a job earning a minimum wage. Options to reduce the tax on labor income include increasing the flat income tax deduction on the personal income tax for low income tax families with one working adult. Options to reduce the payroll tax will depend, however, on actions on several fronts. This includes (i) curbing the abuse of early retirement, disability and sickness benefits; (ii) identifying alternative sources of funding for active labor market programs; and (iii) eliminating the quota-levy system designed originally to encourage the employment of workers with disabilities. Estimates suggest that a 10 percent reduction in payroll taxes would reduce gross wages by around 4 percent and induce about a 2 percent increase in formal employment.

- *Reform the labor market legislation.* The chapter examined five recent proposals for reforming the Polish labor market legislation, indicating where they stand in reaching a balance between modernizing Poland's labor relations without compromising worker's basic rights, including access to social security. These proposals include revisions of labor market legislation concerning temporary contracts, substitute employees, employment in firms with less than 50 employees and payment for overtime work. In most instances, revisions are designed to bring legislation up to date with modern practices. There is one instance, however, where the proposed revision opens scope for abuse and should be reconsidered to avoid this risk. This is the case of the provision allowing the voluntary suspension of binding aspects of the labor code during periods when the employer is in financial distress.

- *Target training programs.* While skills mismatch explains some of the increase in structural unemployment in Poland, the authorities should avoid untargeted training programs. They should focus instead on programs targeting either particular problems (e.g., for skills in short supply), or individuals whose problems are clearly identified and only moderately severe. Better targeting of training programs means focusing training programs on younger adult men and women (25 to 34 years), rather than on older adults and youth. This can be achieved through counseling in the labor offices and better targeting limited public sector resources. Another way to better target limited public sector resources is containing the abuse of tax incentives by higher income tax payers. Tax incentives that allow deduction of personal income tax payments for expenses on education and training benefit disproportionally higher income tax payers.

CHAPTER 5. REFORMING LABOR MARKET PROGRAMS

Introduction[51]

Labor market programs are considered by many in Poland as the first line of defense against unemployment. In 2000, the country spent over 1 percent of GDP on these programs, reaching out to over one million people. While this level of spending is high by the standards of other countries in the region,[52] the recent increase in unemployment has renewed the debate about these programs. Two issues have received the most attention: the balance between passive and active labor market policies, and the recent decision to decentralize the management of active programs to the powiat (county) government level. The two issues are intertwined. The concern about the balance between spending on active and passive labor market programs results from the fact that rising unemployment has crowed out spending on active labor market programs. While this simply reflects budgetary realities, not least because total spending on labor market programs has not declined over the years, many observers blame the increase in unemployment on lower spending on active programs. This view in turns finds support among regional (voivod) and municipal (powiat) self-governments, which are now responsible for a large share of the spending on these active programs.

The experience in Poland and other OECD countries does not indicate that labor market programs are very effective in dealing with unemployment. If anything, the experience indicates that there is considerable risk of creating unemployment traps, where workers facing greater difficulties in the labor market alternate relatively short period of employment (sometimes subsidized employment) with periods receiving unemployment benefits. This is not to say that labor market programs cannot play a role in dealing with unemployment. Labor market programs can make a difference, facilitating the transition out of unemployment, especially for people most likely to be caught in unemployment traps – less-skilled workers, youth, the disabled, and people in high unemployment areas. There is a fine line, however, between providing income support and discouraging job search. The effectiveness of labor market programs should be measured therefore against their ability to reach a balance between providing a safety net while still facilitating the transition back to employment.

---

[51] Labor market programs are carried out by the National Labor Office (NLO) and a network of over 500 municipal (powiat) labor offices (PLO). The majority of the funding (85 percent+) for these programs comes from a 2.45 percent payroll tax earmarked for the Labor Fund, with the remaining coming from the State budget and other sources. There are two forms of passive labor programs in Poland: unemployment benefits and pre-retirement benefits and allowances. The unemployment benefit is available for a finite duration to unemployed workers with a certain period of contribution to the social security system. After exhaustion of the unemployment benefit there is only the means tested general assistance available. The pre-retirement programs are designed for individuals in pre-retirement age and are bridging benefits before an unemployed qualifies for old age pension scheme. They are meant to allow older individuals to withdraw from the labor market before reaching retirement age. The active labor programs include nearly all those available in other OECD countries, such as retraining, public works, intervention programs, loans and employment services. Appendix A at the end of this chapter provides a description of the most important active labor market programs.

[52] Data for the late 1990s indicates that Poland's level of spending on labor market program as a share of GDP is slightly lower than the EU's average (1.2 percent), comparable to Hungary (1.1 percent), and higher than the average for the OECD countries (0.8 percent). Furthermore, the level of spending is much higher than the spending levels in the Czech Republic (0.37 percent) and Estonia (0.2 percent).

It is against this benchmark that this chapter examines Poland's recent experience with labor market programs. It begins by examining recent developments in labor market programs, discussing trends in spending and participation. Next, it reviews several measures for assessing the effectiveness of these programs. The findings suggest that there is a considerable amount of benefit churning, whereby individuals alternate periods receiving unemployment benefits with participation in active labor market programs. Finally, it examines some of the options for reforming labor market programs, drawing from the experience in OECD countries on what appears to work and under which circumstances. The chapter closes with a summary of the main conclusions.

Recent Developments in Labor Market Programs

The most important developments in labor market programs in 1999 and 2000 were the increase in spending on passive programs (unemployment benefits and pre-retirement benefits and allowances), and the partial decentralization of the responsibility for these programs to the voivod and powiat self-governments. While total spending on labor programs have remained constant at around 1 percent of GDP over the years, reaching PLN 6.9 billion in 2000, spending on passive programs accounted for over four-fifths of total spending (Table 5.1). This reflects both the increase in the unemployment rate and ambiguities in the legislation regulating pre-retirement programs, which allowed more applicants for this program than originally anticipated. This problem was compounded by the decentralization of the responsibility for active programs to powait self-governments, since it created additional demands for limited funds at a moment of rising unemployment.

Table 5.1 Labor Fund Expenditure on Labor Market Programs

	1996	1997	1998	1999	2000p
Total expenditure (PLN million)	7,418	6,778	5,011	5,776	6,922
Passive Programs (%)	86.0	76.7	60.0	67.0	81.0
Unemployment benefits	86.0	70.3	46.3	47.0	53.4
Pre-retirement benefits and allowances	0.0	6.4	13.7	20.0	30.8
Active Programs (%)	13.1	21.7	31.5	25.3	19.0
Training	1.2	1.7	2.2	1.8	1.1%
Intervention Works	3.7	4.7	7.1	4.7	2.2
Public Works	2.1	6.2	6.7	3.6	2.1
Graduate Programs	1.7	2.5	4.9	5.1	3.4
Loans	1.1	2.6	4.3	4.0	1.7
Youth Programs	3.1	4.0	6.3	5.5	…
Other Active Programs	0.2	0.1	0.2	0.6	0.5
Other expenditure (%)	0.8	1.7	8.4	7.7	7.9

Source: National Labor Office, and Ministry of Finance (draft budget law). World Bank staff calculations.

Trends in spending on labor market programs. The recent rise in spending on passive programs is widely credited to three factors: the increase in the levels of unemployment, the higher-than-anticipated number of people claiming pre-retirement benefits, and a several very optimistic budget parameters used by the Labor Fund. The budget for 2000 assumed an unemployment scenario (11.5 percent) around 4 percent lower than the actual number of registered unemployed, and a much lower number of people claiming pre-retirement benefits and allowances – lower by as much as 40 percent. This in turn forced the National Labor Office

(NLO) to cut back on active labor market spending, despite the decision earlier in the year to borrow funds from commercial bank to meet some of the Labor Fund's expenditure commitments.

One factor behind the higher-than-anticipated number of people claiming pre-retirement benefits and allowances were relatively lax eligibility criteria. While some of these loopholes had been known for a while, they were fully exploited during this period of rising unemployment. For instance, pre-retirement benefits were designed primarily for unemployed workers who had a working record of 35 years (30 in the case of women) with contributions to the social security system. This however could be reduced to 30 years (25 in the case of women) under special circumstances. These included individuals with at least 15 years of service in the profession considered as special in the Law on Disability and Old Age Pensions,[53] which implied that eligibility could include women at age 41 and men at age 46. Similarly, pre-retirement allowances were designed for individuals eligible for unemployment benefit who had reached 63 years of age (58 years in case of women), and made the required contribution to social security. However, when the employment relationship was terminated for company reasons (restructuring or bankruptcy), the required age was reduced to 55 for women and 60 for men. This could be further reduced to a working record of 35 years in case of women or 40 years in case of men, when the employment relationship had been terminated due to company reasons rather than due to a fault of the employee. This was particularly enticing because pre-retirement allowances were equal to 90 percent of old age pension and could not be lower than the pre-retirement benefit.

To limit the eligibility to and expenditures on pre-retirement programs (expenditures increased over two-thirds in real terms between 1999 and 2000), Parliament introduced two amendments to the legislation governing these programs in December 2000. Eligibility was limited to individuals living in areas with a high unemployment rate. Also, participants would no longer have the option of combining income from work with a pre-retirement benefit and allowance. While this is expected to achieve some reduction in spending, it fails to address some of the most troublesome exceptions (namely the one that allow women at age 41 and men at age 46 to be eligible). Also, it continues to provide an incentive for individuals in high unemployment areas to remain in these areas, blurring the distinction between providing needed income support and creating unemployment and underemployment traps. This is especially true now that these benefits can no longer be combined with income from formal employment.

Similar ambiguities also exist in the rules governing unemployment benefits (Tables 5.2 and 5.3).[54] To be eligible for unemployment benefit (UB), it must be the case that: (i) no job offers are available, no training or retaining is available, no intervention works or public works

---

[53] The list of special jobs includes among others soldiers, teachers, artists and civil servants. Additionally, people who were employed in difficult and dangerous conditions are also considered as special cases and have reduced pre-retirement benefit age requirement.

[54] While the rules set in 1990 provided benefits that varied directly with prior earnings, in October 1992 the monthly unemployment benefit (UB) allowance was set at a uniform nationwide level of 36 percent of the average salary. In 1994 the formula of UB was changed once again. It was set at 260 PLN in 1994 and since then it has been adjusted by the CPI on the quarterly basis. As of September 1, 2000, the base level of monthly UB was 446.70 PLN, which was around 24 percent of the national average wage. Again, the amount and duration of UB varies depending on the work or contribution paying period of an unemployed and the unemployment rate in the particular powiat.

job are available, and no additionally created work places are available, and (ii) in the 12 months before registering as unemployed the claimant worked at least 180 days covered by social insurance. However, the 180-day employment condition is not binding if the claimant falls under certain categories. These include having (i) been laid off by the employer because of economic difficulties; (ii) left school in the last 12 months (recent school graduate); and (iii) been re-employed after a period of collecting unemployment compensation, but the period was shorter than 180 days because of the economic difficulties faced by the employer.[55,56] All three attenuating circumstances were very common in the last two and a half years, and probably contributed to the increase in applications for unemployment benefits.

Table 5.2 Amount of Unemployment Benefit

% of the base level	Work/Contribution paying period
80%	Less than 5 years
100%	5-20 years
120%	More than 20 years

Source: National Labor Office.

Table 5.3: Duration of Unemployment Benefit

Duration	Requirements
6 months	Unemployment rate in powiat is less than the national average
12 months	Unemployment rate in powiat is higher than the national average
18 months	Unemployment rate in powiat exceeds twice national average and the contribution paying period of an unemployed is at least 20 years; or the unemployed has at least one child not older than 15 years and the spouse is unemployed and has no right for the UB

Source: National Labor Office.

Participation in active programs. Despite the increase spending on passive labor market programs, participants in active programs still account for over half of the around one million people involved in Poland's labor programs over the last few years (Table 5.4). Intervention works have been the most popular among the active labor market programs, accounting for around one third of all participants. Graduate programs grew the most in terms of popularity, reaching over 20 percent of all participants by 1999, up from just over 7 percent when they were first established. The main passive labor market program, unemployment benefits, saw its numbers steadily declined between 1996 and 1998 along with the overall decline in unemployment. The increase in unemployment that began in 1999 pushed participation up

---

[55] Other conditions under which claimants are exempt from the 180-day employment condition include having been (i) recently released from the military; (ii) recently been receiving a recovery or disability allowance; and (iii) recently been released from a penal institution.

[56] Unemployment benefits are payable starting the first day after benefits are claimed. If birth is given during the period of unemployment compensation an extension is granted. Unemployment compensation is denied or suspended if an unemployed person (i) has refused to accept a valid offer of work, retraining, participation in intervention or public works; (ii) has terminated or caused termination of an employment contract within 6 months before registration in the local labor office; (iii) stays abroad for more than 30 days or remains in other situation causing lack of readiness to take up employment. The standard benefit denial period is 90 days. A claimant, who has received a payment in error, must repay the over payment within 14 days from the day of receiving notice from a municipal (powiat) labor office.

again, although not to the same levels because an increasing number of unemployed are taking advantage of pre-retirement programs.[57]

Table 5.4 Number of Labor Market Programs Participants, 1996-99 (in '000)

	1996	1997	1998	1999
UB recipients[a]	1,374.4	862.7	405.4	496.6
Active Programs Participants	367.3	611.3	547.2	559.3
Training	86.0	139.1	138.2	136.5
Intervention Works	139.6	174.5	149.9	167.5
Public Works	106.2	151.0	106.3	75.8
Graduate Programs	28.1	134.6	139.6	169.0
Loans[b]	7.4	12.1	13.0	10.4

a) Yearly average number of unemployed eligible for the unemployment benefits.
b) Number of jobs created on the basis of loans.
Source: National Labor Office.

The Labor Fund's financial difficulties. The increase in pre-retirement benefits and allowances, plus the higher than expected increase in unemployment, were the principal causes behind the PLN 1.3 billion deficit in the operations of the Labor Fund. The deficit was covered by a PLN 750 million loan taken by the Labor Fund, a PLN 100 million transfer from the state budget, and PLN 450 million reallocated within the Labor Fund from resources originally assigned to active labor market programs. While this emergency funding allowed the Labor Fund to cover its deficit in 2000, it implies that almost no funds will be available for active labor market programs in 2001. The reason is that powiats are entitled to receive between PLN 400 and 600 million in additional funds to compensate the funding that was withdrawn from active labor market programs in 2000. This results from the fact that contracts signed between the powiats and the National Labor Office were canceled after many powiats had already assumed commitments with prospective employers for several months (commitments to co-finance employees salaries). Powiats were therefore forced to meet these commitments from their own funds, and now need to be refunded. The funds that will be transferred to powiats this year are more or less the funding that is available for active labor market programs in the 2001 budget.

Decentralization. It is against the backdrop of rising unemployment and financial difficulties for the Labor Fund that the decentralization of labor market programs has occurred. Since January 2000 the subnational levels of government -- voivod self governments and powiat self governments -- have gained increased responsibility for carrying out active labor market programs.[58] This decentralization, giving subnational governments the responsibility for initiating and managing active program, and leaving with the National Labor Office (NLO) and its voivod offices the responsibility for planning, monitoring and evaluating these programs, allowed the NLO to retain the responsibility for allocating 50 percent of the funds available for active programs, even if services are still being provided by the powiat labor offices.

---

[57] The increase in the number of beneficiaries of unemployment benefits did not alter, however, the declining coverage of those registered as unemployed.
[58] The new division of responsibilities was defined in the January 1, 2000 Act on Employment and Counteracting Unemployment.

The procedures for allocating the 50 percent of funds managed by the NLO are similar to those used before the new assignment of responsibilities in early 2000. The NLO signs individual contracts with the powiats covering the range of services to be provided, and defines standard measures of performance in the delivery of these services. For the remaining 50 percent, the powiats receive resources from the Labor Fund according to an algorithm. This algorithm defines that total transfers must include funding for payment of entitlements under passive programs (unemployment and pre-retirement benefits), as well as funding for active measures and for covering administrative costs (e.g., computer systems, dissemination efforts, and research and analysis). The funding available for active programs is a function of the ratio of number of registered unemployed in the given powiat and in the rest of the country, adjusted to account for the shares of long term unemployed and of youth unemployed in this universe of registered unemployed.[59] Similarly, the funding available to cover administrative costs (e.g., computer equipment, dissemination, research and analysis) is a function of the ratio between registered unemployed in the powiat and total universe of registered unemployed, without making adjustments for long term and youth unemployment.

While the details in the implementation of this decentralization process are still being worked out, it has come under attack from two fronts. Opponents have argued that there is already a policy-induced segmentation of the labor market, whereby unemployed workers in rural areas are encouraged to stay in those areas. The further segmentation to powiats will only exacerbate the problem. Also, under the current system, decentralization does not allow the smooth management of funds. The moment contracts are signed between the NLO and the powiats, funds are looked and cannot be reallocated for other needs. This, for instances, was one of the factors contributing to the Labor Fund's financial difficulties in 2000.

The Polish authorities appear committed, however, to the underlying principle governing the decentralization process, namely the delegation of decision-making responsibility to subnational governments. To this end, they have already begun correcting some of the main problems with the current system. The information used to guide the allocation of resources is being improved, with quarterly labor force surveys now providing unemployment figures by voivodship, as opposed to national averages only. An independent measurement of unemployment will reduce the incentive for local labor office to encourage unemployed workers to register and, therefore, increase their share of funding. This should also encourage greater accountability, as indicators of unemployment will become more comparable across voivodships.

---

[59] The algorithm for this allocation is the following: Ap= Pi*((Lp*Wa*Wb*Wc*Wd)/Lk); where Ap represents the funding budgeted by the Labor Fund for carrying out active labor market policies, minus the funding left at the disposal of the Chairman of the National Labor Office. The parameters between the brackets are the following: Lp is the number of unemployed persons registered in powiat, as for 30 June of the preceding year; Wa is an adjusting coefficient that takes into account the unemployment rate in the given powiat, as for 30 June of the preceding year – varies between 1.0 to 1.8; Wb is the adjusting coefficient that takes into account the share of the long-term unemployed (over 12 months) persons in the universe of the total number of unemployed persons registered in the given powiat, as for 30 June of the preceding year – it varies between 1.0 to 1.3; Wc is the adjusting coefficient that takes into account the share of the unemployed persons no longer eligible for a benefit in the total number of unemployed persons registered in the given powiat, as for 30 June of the preceding year – it varies between 1.0 to 1.3; and Wd is the adjusting coefficient that takes into account the share of unemployed persons aged 24 years or under in the total number of unemployed persons registered in a given powiat as for 30 June of the preceding year – it varies between 1.0 to 1.3. And Lk is the total number of unemployed persons registered in all powiats, adjusted by coefficient Wa-Wd for 30 June of the preceding year.

Finally, there might be the option of allowing reallocation of funds within voivodships. This was, for instance, possible under the previous system, where the Voivod Labor Office could shift funds for active programs from surplus to deficit areas in the 3rd quarter of the fiscal year. This however requires better indicators for assessing the effectiveness of labor market programs. We turn therefore to this topic next.

Assessing Labor Market Programs

The decentralization of responsibilities for labor market programs, coupled with the rise in unemployment, has brought new attention to the need for assessing the effectiveness of the labor market programs, identifying what works and under which circumstances. Under the previous centralized arrangement, the National Labor Office had been collecting information on the effectiveness of active programs, keeping detailed account of the unit costs of programs and the percentage of participants finding a job within the first three months of leaving these programs. This information helped guide the allocation of resources, especially since these indicators were embedded in the contracts signed between the NLO and the powiats. The downside was that these indicators also created wrong incentives, such as encouraging labor offices to extend training to those most likely to find employment upon completion of the programs, keeping unit costs down and increasing the success rate.

This section assesses labor market programs in Poland, measuring them against three broadly defined performance indicators. First, it considers the performance indicators used by the National Labor Office,[60] comparing the difference performance of selected programs, and assessing the incentives embedded in these indicators. Next, it examines indicators estimating the degree of dependence created by these programs, as measured by the extend of 'benefit churning' and the reliance on unemployment benefits as a substitute for social assistance. Finally, it calculates the degree of targeting of these programs, identifying the main characteristics of unemployment benefit recipients, and the extent to which benefits flow to those in greater need.

NLO Indicators. Under the oversight of the National Labor Office the effectiveness of active labor market program were, and to a lesser degree still are, measured against two indicators: the unit cost of the program per participant and the percentage of participants finding a job after the program. Table 5.5 presents figures for these two indicators for selected programs during the period 1996 to 1999. The figures suggest that training was the most effective, with declining unit costs and more than 40 percent of participants finding a job after participation in the program. Intervention works and graduate programs come next, with high rates of after program job placement, and declining unit costs, albeit from a slightly higher level. These three programs compared favorably with public works, which had higher unit costs and much lower after program job placement rates.

---

[60] The unit costs of programs and the rate of post-program employment of the participants in active labor market programs.

Table 5.5 Effectiveness of Selected Active Labor Market Programs (%)

	Unit costs in PLN				Percentage of participants finding a job			
	1996	1997	1998	1999	1996	1997	1998	1999
Training	1,076	825	780	768	55.5	49.0	51.8	50.6
Intervention Works	1,982	1,822	2,366	1,624	50.6	56.8	64.1	65.1
Public Works	1,436	2,764	3,153	2,746	8.2	7.1	11.8	13.2
Graduate Programs	4,519	1,252	1,750	1,748	0.0	68.9	72.7	57.1

Source: National Labor Office.

While these two indicators provide some measure of the cost effectiveness of the programs, they are unable to capture either deadweight losses or substitution effects. A deadweight loss occurs when, for instance, a worker who would have found a job in any event participates in one these programs, taking away resources that could be made available to someone in greater need. This is particularly a problem because the two indicators used by the National Labor Office encourage powiat labor office to select among the applicants that are more likely to find a job upon completion of the program. Candidates that are more employable are likely to exit the program earlier, keeping unit costs down and increasing the percentage of participants that find a job. The substitution effect occurs when a job created through these programs comes at the expense of the job of another worker, who did not go through training or receive an employment subsidy (intervention and graduate programs). To illustrate the magnitude that these deadweight losses and substitution effects can reach, recent evaluations made for programs in selected OECD countries (Australia, Belgium, Ireland and the Netherlands) indicate that the combined deadweight losses and substitution effects in intervention and graduate programs reached, in some instances, as much as 90 percent. This implies that for every 100 jobs created only 10 were considered net gains in employment.[61]

Another factor that is not readily captured from these two indicators is the incentive faced by employers under these schemes. The Labor Fund reimburses the employer at different rates depending on the program (Table 5.6). This affects the preference of each employer (e.g., private enterprise, powiat administration), as well as the unit costs of each program. Not surprisingly, the costs of public works are higher than for other programs, not least because the reimbursement rates are over three times higher than for the two other programs. It is also interesting to observe that under decentralized management of active labor market programs, powiats show greater interest in public work,[62] despite the fact that program evaluations indicate this is the least effective program in facilitating the transition back to employment.

---

[61] Although the OECD evidence also suggests that it is possible to raise the net employment gains of these programs via targeting of particular groups among the unemployed and close monitoring of employer behavior to curb abuses.

[62] An interview with an official from a voivodship labor office, he indicated that powiats had three incentives to encourage applications for public works. It subsidizes labor for public works carried out from their own budgets (e.g., road maintenance). It reduces the demand for social assistance, since claimants of social assistance benefits are, in many instances, the same as the participants in public works. And the reimbursement from the Labor Fund is higher. The official also indicated that many of the civil servants working for the powiat administration had been hired under public works programs, allowing a hidden increase in public administration.

Table 5.6 Selected Labor Programs: Maximum Reimbursement Rates[1]

Program	Reimbursement Amount (PLN)[2]	Reimbursements (% of minimum wage)
Intervention programs	527	75.0
Public works	1,653	236.0
Graduate programs	527	75.0

1) One month of full-time work.
2) Includes salary and social insurance contributions.
Source: National Labor Office.

Independent evaluations of Polish labor market programs indicate that, even when one accounts for deadweight losses, the ranking of labor market programs is not very different from the one that results from the analysis of the two indicators provided by the National Labor Office, although there are some important qualifications. For instance, research by O'Leary (1998) using quasi-experimental methods[63] indicates that intervention programs, loan for self-employed, and retraining are the most effective in raising the participants chances of getting into a regular job. The same however cannot be said about employment services, which had no measurable impact, and public works, which showed a negative impact on participants' future employment opportunities (Table 5.7).

Table 5.7 Assessment of the Effectiveness of Labor Market Programs Using Quasi-Experimental Methods

Program	Net impact	Comments
Intervention programs	Positive	26% increase in the probability of ever finding a normal job.
Loans for self employed	Positive	29% increase in the probability of getting into a normal job or non-subsidized self-employment.
Retraining	Positive	Comparing participants and non-participants, 12% more of the participants got into non-subsidized employment, with a PLN 23 gain in average salary. Prime-aged workers, with non-vocational background benefited the most from the program.
Employment services	Insignificant	Estimated impact on employment outcomes was small and not statistically significant.
Public works	Negative	Reduced the chances of getting into a normal job ever by 5% and by 8% during the observed period.

Source: O'Leary (1998).

Benefit churning and dependence. The impact of these programs, even those that show a positive impact, is mitigated however by what Jochen et al. (1999) call 'benefit churning'.[64] They indicate that participation in intervention programs and public works is, in many instances, an intermediate stage between two spells of unemployment benefits.[65] This appears to be

[63] The quasi-experimental method consists of assessing the impact of the program on employment and earnings by comparing active labor market program participants with the most similar person from the unemployment register of the same labor office who did not participate in one of these programs.

[64] To ensure that the results reflect the true impact of the program, they compare participants and non-participants who have the same observable characteristics and an identical labor market history. Also, they only compare persons who find themselves in an identical phase of the transition cycle, ensuring that the results are not influenced by differences in the macroeconomic environment. The latter is an improvement over the quasi-experimental method employed by O'Leary (1998).

[65] This happens because workers are entitled to unemployment benefits if they have worked at least 180 days in the preceding year.

particularly the case for males heads of households, who, in their words, 'were seen by labor office officials as particularly worthy of prolonged income support from the state'.

The findings of Jochen, et al. (1999) are supported by earlier research by Gora and Schmidt (1998) on income support for the long term unemployed. They find that unemployment benefits account for an important share of the income of the long term (over one year) and very long term unemployed (over two years), despite the requirement of at least 180 days of work in the previous 12 months. During the period 1992-95 unemployment benefits accounted on average for just under 40 percent of the income of those who had been unemployed for less than one year, which is the target group for unemployment benefits.[66] During this same period, unemployment benefits accounted for around 20 percent of the income of the long-term unemployed and about 15 percent of the income of the very long-term unemployed. Even under the conservative assumption that the income of these different groups (unemployed, long term and the very long term unemployed) is the same, this suggests that around 60 percent of the recipients of unemployment benefits continued drawing on these benefits in the second year, with the ratio falling to 39 percent in the third year.

Gora and Schimidt (1998) also report that social assistance and other transfers accounted for around 7 percent of the income of long term and very long term unemployed, which is less than half of the contribution of unemployment benefits to the household's income. They conclude therefore that unemployment benefits did substitute social assistance in providing income support to the poor during this period. While this provides some support to the notion that there is indeed "benefit churning", it also points to another measure against which policymakers need to assess the effectiveness of labor market programs: the degree of targeting to those in greater need.

Targeting.[67] Many of the reforms of labor market programs introduced during the 1990s aimed at targeting unemployment benefits to the actual needs of the poor and vulnerable. Eligibility was gradually tightened and the effective replacement rate lowered, reducing program costs and, given the budget constraint, reaching a larger share of the poor. Indeed, while unemployment benefits are not means tested, most of the recipients are very poor. Almost two-thirds of the households with members receiving unemployment benefits are at the bottom 10 percent (decile) of the expenditure distribution. For these households, unemployment benefits contribute about 15 percent toward closing the poverty gap.[68]

---

[66] The sample in Gora and Schmidt (1998) excludes widowed and divorced men and women.

[67] The high degree of targeting of unemployment benefits should not indicate that its an effective manner of dealing with poverty. Unemployment benefits are paid primarily to the unemployed, and poverty is related to other factors, in particular the number of dependents (usually children) in the households. The risk of falling and staying in poverty increases with number of children under the age of 15 in the household. The social assistance offices indicates that unemployment is a key indicator for eligibility to social transfers. Among the very poor (bottom decile of the expenditure distribution) the mean social assistance doubles for households with unemployed members, even if the household also receives unemployment benefits (38 percent increase).

[68] The poverty gap measures the difference between the household's per capita expenditure and the upper limit of the decile's per capita expenditure. The following scales were used to express equivalent units: 1.0 for the household head, 0.7 for other adults, and 0.5 for a child under 14.

The main difficulty is distinguishing whether this degree of targeting of the poor reflects tighter eligibility criteria or self-selection on the part of those receiving benefits. For instance, most of the unemployment benefits, both in relative and absolute numbers, go to households in small towns (less than 20,000) and villages in rural areas. Together residents in these areas account for almost two-thirds of all the households receiving unemployment benefits, even though they account for just over 50 percent of the registered unemployed. This suggest that eligibility rules for unemployment benefits may not be strictly enforced in these areas, encouraging households with unemployed members to remain in small towns and villages in rural areas.

There might be also a large degree of self-selection by less-skilled workers. Almost three-quarters of those receiving unemployment benefits have educational attainment equivalent to basic vocational education or less. This indicates that less-skilled workers, who are unemployed, are more likely to register as unemployed and receive benefits. This is remarkable given that many of the unemployed with basic vocational education or less are also long term unemployed and, therefore, are not longer eligible for benefits. This could provide additional support to the notion that there is indeed 'benefit churning', where less-skilled workers re-enter the labor market only for enough time to become eligible for unemployment benefits again. This incentive appears to be particularly strong in high unemployment areas, where eligibility has been extended to 18 months.

In summary, the assessment of the effectiveness of active labor market programs suggests that there is considerable scope for improvements in the design and implementation of these programs. This ranges from reducing deadweight loss and displacement effects to improving targeting of the poor without creating unemployment traps. The latter is by far the greatest challenge for policymakers, especially in an increasingly decentralized system. Labor market programs have progressively targeted rural areas and less-skilled workers, who in turn have become increasingly dependent on these benefits. We turn next therefore to the options available for reforming labor market programs.

Options for Reforming Labor Market Programs

Decentralization. The main issue facing labor market programs in Poland is how to continue implementing the decentralization process approved in January 2000. The challenge is to minimize wrong incentives on the part of the officials registering unemployed workers, such as over-registration to attract more funding, while still delegating some decision-making responsibility to those implementing these programs. The government has moved to improve information on regional unemployment rates, making the labor force survey representative at the voivodship level, and reducing the reliance on information from local labor offices. Additional actions need to be taken, however, to ensure that the principles of targeting and accountability that guide decentralization are not achieved at the expense of a minimum efficient scale in managing labor market programs.

The options to achieve this balance between decentralization and economies of scale in service delivery include the following:

- *Contracting out the delivery of labor market programs.* Economies of scale in the delivery of labor market programs can be achieved by contracting out the delivery of these services to the private sector, since one provider can meet the needs of more than one powiat. Private provision also increases competition, reducing administrative costs and, in some instances, allowing cost recovery. Private provision of these services should also include private sector labor intermediation. Labor contractors can play an important role in an environment of increase labor rotation, especially if individuals are not familiar with the process of applying for jobs, and employers are not familiar with a process of selecting workers from a more ample pool of applicants. In many countries private sector labor intermediation has proven to be important in the process of transformation of agriculture and the increase in the volume of production, particularly in fruits and vegetables where producers depend on substantial seasonal labor.

- *Defining common standards in the delivery of services.* The reliance on outside contractors for the delivery of labor market programs will require clearer service delivery standards and better designed performance indicators. Otherwise, there is a risk of perpetuating the deadweight losses associated with these programs, whereby candidates with better chances of finding a job are targeted. Options to improve targeting include focusing on unemployed workers with less than secondary education in high unemployment areas. Options for performance indicators include ensuring that participants in labor market programs do not engage in 'benefit churning', continuously rotating between programs.

- *Separating sources of funding for active and passive programs.* One of the main constraints for the implementation of the decentralization of labor market programs has been the competition between active and passive programs. This has lead many policymakers and policy observers to call for a re-balancing the level of spending, increasing the share of active labor market programs. The argument is usually presented in the following way: 'why should society pay the unemployed to be idle when these public funds could be used instead to supply them with a range of labor market services that could raise their chance of getting a job?' The answer is that rising unemployment leads automatically to an increase in spending on passive labor market programs because these are entitlements. Active labor market programs, which are funded by the same payroll tax, are discretionary spending, and therefore are automatically crowed out because there is an overall ceilings on spending given by payroll tax revenues. One option to get around this problem is to define separate sources of funding for active and passive labor market programs. Passive labor market programs would continue to be funded by the payroll tax, albeit at a lower rate, while active programs would receive funding from general revenues. This would reduce competition between active and passive labor market policies, reducing concerns that spending on active programs plunge exactly when unemployment is rising. This would also allow decentralization to proceed without disruptions.

Balancing passive and active labor market programs. The other important issue facing labor market program in Poland is achieving greater complementarity between active and passive programs. The challenge here is moving toward a better balance between active and passive programs, without compromising progress achieved in targeting those most vulnerable. This last point is particularly contentious because, if a better balance between active and passive labor market programs is to be achieved, neither can passive labor market programs substitute for social assistance, nor can active programs play the role of income support. This in turns requires recognizing that any measure to improve the effectiveness of these programs will need to deal with the fact that labor market programs play and will continue to play an important social assistance function, especially since poverty is closely associated with unemployment.

The following paragraphs draw lessons from the experience of other OECD countries to indicate options for reform. These range from measures to improve the design of active labor market programs to adding re-employment bonuses to encourage early exit from passive programs. While these actions should reduce deadweight loss and displacement effects, their impact in generating new job opportunities will be limited without the implementation of policies for job creation discussed in the previous chapter. The reason is simple, if an economy is generating few job vacancies, it should be no surprised that active measures are relatively ineffective. There is hope nevertheless that improvements in labor market programs aimed at minimizing the problems of deadweight loss and displacement identified above could still lead to better targeting of those in greatest need.

Improving program effectiveness. The evidence from other OECD countries indicates that there are two crucial features in the design of labor market programs that enhance their effectiveness:

- Relying as much as possible on job-finding incentives and job-search assistance. This in turn should be combined with measures to increase monitoring of job search effort and enforcement of work tests.

- Encouraging early intervention, reaching back to the time when disadvantage groups are still in school. This includes steps to reduce early school leaving, and ensure that students leave school with basic skills and competencies.

These general recommendations can be broken down further into more specific advice on how to improve program design and targeting:

- *Adding re-employment bonuses*. The experience in some OECD countries[69] indicates that when job search assistance is combined with re-employment bonuses there is a significant reduction in the average duration of unemployment. The logic here is that workers will increase their job search effort before the end of their unemployment benefit period because of the financial incentive. Also, since the employment subsidy is going to the worker rather than the employer, this reduces the risk of job displacement. The only issue the authorities need to safeguard against is the incentive for workers (in agreement with the employers) to abuse the system by deliberately asking to be laid off to collect the bonus once they are re-employed. One way of

---

[69] Japan, Korea, and the United States.

implementing this recommendation in a fiscally responsible fashion is to allow unemployment benefit recipients who find a job within the first six months of unemployment to keep a share of what they would have been entitled to receive during the remaining period.

- *Including an on-the-job component.* Since the purpose of active programs is to facilitate the transition back into employment, they tend to be most effective when they include an on-the-job component. This includes internships for training and re-training programs, and are usually best achieved by establishing strong links with local employers. While this on-the-job component cannot ensure against displacing other workers who did not benefit from training, it does help in reducing the deadweight loss, whereby participants would have found a job regardless of whether they went through the program.

- *Making early interventions.* The experience in Poland and other OECD countries is that early intervention can make a difference in mitigating the risks of structural unemployment among certain disadvantaged groups. This is especially the case in Poland, where employers are placing greater emphasis on workers having the appropriate skills. The design of these programs usually relies on very close targeting and financial incentives for the participants. One example that should be encouraged is the programs currently being implemented to mitigate the risk of structural unemployment in rural areas by 'Improving Educational Opportunities of Children from the Former State Farm Settlements'. The main purpose of this program is to allow the greatest possible number of children from former state farm employees to continue their education and graduate from secondary school. The program provides scholarships to children from former state farm employees, and children from families living in the state farm settlements, with a per capita income lower than 70 percent of the minimum wage. The scholarships can be used for food, housing, commuting to school, buying textbooks, and school fees.[70]

Avoiding unemployment traps. The reform of labor market programs would not be complete without measures to avoid unemployment and underemployment traps. Chief among these measures would be tightening eligibility to pre-retirement benefits and allowances, so that only eligible unemployed workers 60 years old or older would be entitled to this benefit. This would both avoid abuse under the current system, and discourage individuals in high unemployment areas from staying behind on the expectation of one day becoming eligible. Another measure would be to increase the flat income tax deduction on the personal income tax for low-income families, increasing their net labor income and encouraging them to continue working. Finally, as mentioned above, there is the need to better monitor job search and provide re-employment bonuses to encourage early leave from the labor market programs.

---

[70] Another message from this example is the need to consider incremental investments, especially those that provide incentives for students to stay in school.

Conclusions

This chapter reviews Poland's recent experience with labor market programs. The review included an account of recent developments, especially the factors contributing to the increase in spending on passive labor market programs and their implications for the decentralization of these programs. It also included an assessment of the effectiveness of labor market programs, focusing on measures of cost-effectiveness and adequate targeting of the poor. Finally, the review focused on options for reforming these programs to effectively complete the decentralization process and, in doing so, achieve a greater complementarity between passive and active labor market programs.

The two most important factors contributing to the recent increase in spending on passive programs were the increase in unemployment and relatively easy access to unemployment benefits and pre-retirement programs, especially in high unemployment areas. As a result, spending on passive labor market programs increase by over two-thirds in real terms between 1999 and 2000, despite the fact that unemployment rose by less that one-fifth. Higher spending on passive labor market programs crowed out spending on active programs, derailing the decentralization process. This happened because funds that were originally earmarked for active programs implemented by powiat labor offices were temporarily withdrawn to partially cover a deficit in the operations of the Labor Fund. The combination of rising unemployment, relatively easy access to benefits, and the powiat labor office's incentives to encourage unemployment registration only contributed to accentuate the imbalance between active and passive labor market programs.

The challenge now for policymakers is to re-establish this balance without compromising progress in targeting programs to those in greatest need. To achieve this balance, the chapter makes the following recommendations:

- *Contracting out the delivery of active labor market programs.* This should allow decentralization to proceed without sacrificing economies of scale in the delivery of labor market programs, since one provider can meet the needs of more than one powiat. Private provision also increases competition, reducing administrative costs and, in some instances, allowing cost recovery. Private provision of these services should also include private sector labor intermediation, since private labor contractors tend to be more familiar with labor market developments. This however can only be achieved if there are clearer service delivery standards and better designed performance indicators for the delivery of these services. Otherwise, there is a risk of abusing the system and perpetuating the deadweight losses associated with these programs. Options for targeting include unemployed workers with less than secondary education in high unemployment areas. Options for performance indicators include reducing dependency on these labor market programs.

- *Add re-employment bonuses.* The experience in some OECD countries[71] indicates that combining job search assistance with re-employment bonuses significantly reduces the average duration of unemployment. The logic here is that workers will

---

[71] Japan, Korea, and the United States.

increase their job search effort before the end of their unemployment benefit period because of the financial incentive. Also, since the employment subsidy is going to the worker rather the employer, it reduces the risk of job displacement. One way of implementing this recommendation is to allow unemployment benefit recipients who find a job within the first six months of unemployment to keep a share of what they were entitled to receive during this period.

- *Separate sources of funding.* Defining separate sources of funding for active and passive labor market programs would reduce competition between programs, especially during periods of rising unemployment. The proposed option is that passive labor market programs continue to be funded by the payroll tax, albeit at a lower rate, while active programs would receive funding from general revenues.

- *Tighten eligibility criteria for pre-retirement programs.* To avoid so-called unemployment traps, the eligibility for pre-retirement programs should be limited to unemployed workers 60 years old or older. This would both avoid abuse under the current system, and discourage individuals in high unemployment areas from staying behind on the expectation of one day becoming eligible. Another measure to encourage low-income workers to remain employed would be to increase the flat income tax deduction on the personal income tax for low-income families and increasing their net labor income.

ANNEX A: AN OVERVIEW OF ACTIVE LABOR MARKET PROGRAMS

This annex provides a brief description of the most important active labor market programs available in Poland. These include nearly all those available in other OECD countries, most notably retraining, public works, intervention and graduate programs, loans and employment services:

- *Retraining.* The retraining of unemployed workers provides an additional short term job skill training to make job seekers ready to fill job openings in the region. The cost of training cannot exceed two average wages and should not last longer than 6 months. Retraining participants receive a stipend that amounts to 20 percent of the unemployment benefit.

- *Public Works.* The public works program is a short-term (up to 12 months) direct job creation program with employment on projects organized by government agencies including municipal governments. Local Labor Office (LLO) for up to 6 months refunds wages of hired unemployed up to the level of 75 percent of the national average wage[72] plus social insurance contribution. Alternatively LLO may refund up to 100 percent of average wage and social insurance contribution for a period of 12 months for every second month. The wage level makes clear the main aim of public works, which is an income transfer. The secondary aims of the program are to maintain job readiness skills of the unemployed and to contribute to the public health and infrastructure.

- *Intervention Programs.* The intervention works program is much like the public works program, except that either public agencies or private firms may operate the projects. The refund is set be equal to the Unemployment Benefit (UB) and it is paid for six months. Another available option is that LLO refunds up to the level of minimum wage for 12 months, every second month. There are also incentives for employers to permanently retain workers. After the end of an Intervention Works project which may last up to six months, employers can receive one off wage subsidy for retained workers amounting to up to 150 percent of the national average wage. The low project wages and the incentive for continued employment mean that Intervention Works operates essentially as a wage subsidy program.

- *Graduate programs.* The graduate program is similar to intervention works, with the exception that it is targeted only for school graduates, i.e., those unemployed who graduated from school within the last 12 months. The Labor Fund refunds for up to 12 months the costs incurred by the employer, but the subsidy may not exceed the amount of unemployment benefit. Social security contribution is also covered by the Labor Fund. The objective of graduate program is to create opportunity for graduates

---

[72] The national average wage is determined quarterly by the Central Statistical Office (GUS) and is based on earnings in selected core industries and occupations.

to get experience and on-job training to improve their labor market situation in the future. There is an incentive provided to employers for keeping the graduates employed after 12 months of the program. The Labor Fund covers the social insurance contribution for additional 12 months for each graduate employed.

- *Loans.* The loans are provided for employers who create jobs for the unemployed for at least two years, and for unemployed individuals who are interest in setting up their own business. The maximum loan is small with the maximum size limited to 20 times the national average wage. Loans are made market rates of interest and must be repaid immediately in full if the planned enterprise is not initiated. A strong incentive for business survival is provided by a 50 percent loan principal reduction granted to businesses that survive at least two years.

- *Special programs.* These programs are aimed at risk groups and should not exceed 10 percent of the amount allocated for active labor market policies. These risk groups include the long-term unemployment, women, youth under 24 years of age, workers laid off from enterprises undergoing restructuring, unemployed in rural areas. These special programs provide many of the services available in the programs defined above (training, wage and payroll tax refunds, loans), although in many instances under more favorable conditions. For instance, interest rates on loans can be reduced to zero under certain conditions.

- *Employment services (ES).* The employment service is the central function of local labor offices. Local labor offices are one-stop-shop for reemployment assistance. These offices act as a unified clearinghouse for referral to a variety of active and passive support. The ES offers a full range of placement services including job interview referral, counseling, skills assessment, job search training, resume preparation, and job clubs.

REFERENCES

Andrews, E. and Thomas Hoopengardner, 1999, "Disability and Work in Poland", mimeo, World Bank.

Arellano, M. and S. Bond, 1991, "Some tests of specification for panel data: Monte Carlo evidence and an application to employment equations", *Review of Economic Studies*, 58(2): 277-297.

Baldwin, R., 1995, "The effect of trade and foreign direct investment on employment and relative wages", NBER Working Paper 5037, February, National Bureau of Economic Research, Cambridge.

Bedi A. S., 1998, "Sector choice, multiple job holding and wage differentials: evidence from Poland", *The Journal of Development Studies*, October.

Bell, Una-Louise, 2000, "Mobility in transition: the case of Poland", ZEW, Germany, processed.

Bentolila, Samuel, 1997, *Polish Labor Market Institutions on the Road to the EU*, Madrid: Centro de Estuydios Monetaros y Financieros. Working Paper # 9712

Berman, E., J. Bound and Z. Griliches, 1994, "Changes in the demand for skilled labor within U.S. manufacturing: evidence from the annual survey of manufactures", *Quarterly Journal of Economics*, CIX (2): 367-397.

Bernard, A. B. and J.B. Jensen, 1999, "Exceptional exporter performance: cause, effect, or both?", *Journal of International Economics*, 47: 1-25.

Bernard, A. B. and C. Jones, 1996, Productivity across industries and countries: time series theory and evidence, *Review of Economics and Statistics*, 78(1): 135-46.

Cavalcanti, C., 2000, "Concept Paper for the Poland Labor Market Study – The Challenge of Job Creation", mimeo, World Bank, Washington, DC.

Cavalcanti, C. and Zhicheng Li, 2000, "Reforming Tax Expenditure Programs in Poland", October, World Bank Policy Research Working Paper 2465, Washington, DC.

Chlon, Agnieska, 1998, "Does Unemployment Influence Migration in Poland?" The Warsaw School of Economics, Warsaw.

Chlon, Agnieska, 2000, "The Polish Farmers' Social Security System", mimeo, Warsaw.

Cohany, Sharon, 1998, "Worker in alternative employment arrangements: a second look," *Monthly Labor Review* 121 (11): 3-21.

Cohany, Sharon, 1996, "Workers in alternative employment arrangements," *Monthly Labor Review* 119 (10): 31-45

Davis, S. and J. Haltiwanger J., 1990, "Gross Job Creation and Destruction: Microeconomic Evidence and Macroeconomic Implications", NBER Macroeconomic Annual 5: 123-168, National Bureau of Economic Research, Cambridge.

den Haan, Wouter, Garey Ramey, and Joel Watson, 2000, "Job Destruction and Propagation of Shocks," *American Economic Review*, June, 90(3): 482-498.

Faggio, Giulia and Jozef Konings, 1999, "Gross Job Flows and Firm Growth in Transition Countries: Evidence on Five Countries", CEPR Discussion Paper No. 2261. CEPR, London.

FAO (Food and Agriculture), 1999, *Polish Agriculture: Economic Transition and Long Run Trends* (June draft), Rome.

Frenkel, Izasław, and Andrzej Rosner, 2000, "Population and Labor Market in Rural Poland," manuscript.

Gora, M. and Christof Schmidt, 1998, Long-term unemployment, unemployment benefits and social assistance: the Polish experience, *Empirical Economics*, 23 (1/2): 55-85.

Greenaway, D., R.C. Hine and P. Wright, 1999, An empirical assessment of the impact of trade on employment in the United Kingdom, *European Journal of Political Economy*, 15: 485-500.

Gregory, M. and C. Greenhalgh, 1997, "International trade, de-industrialisation and labour demand: an input-output study for the UK 1979-1990", In: Borkakoti, J. and C.R. Milner (Eds.), 1997, *International Trade and Labour Markets*, London: Mcmillan.

GUS (Polish Central Statistical Office), 1998, "The situation in the Rural Labor Market with special consideration of individual farmers", Warsaw.

GUS (Polish Central Statistical Office),1992-1999, Labor Force Survey (several), Warsaw.

Haltiwanger, John, 2000, "Aggregate Growth: What Have We Learned from Microeconomic Evidence?", University of Maryland, College Park, processed.

Haskel, J.E. and M.J. Slaughter, 1998, "Does the sector bias of skill-biased technological change explain changing wage inequality?", NBER Working Paper, 6565, May. NBER, Cambridge, Massachusetts.

Hipple, Stephen, 1998, "Contingent Work: Results from the second survey", *Monthly Labor Review* 121(11): 22-30.

Jochen, K., Hartmut Lehmann, Christof Schimidt, 1999, "Active Labor Market Programs in Poland: Human Capital Enhancement, Stigmatization or Benefit Churning", Allgemeines Statistisches Archiv, 83, 161-169.

Kwiatkowski, Eugeniusz, Pawel Kubiak and Leszek Kucharski, 2000, "Inter-industry and intra-industry mobility of labour in Poland in 1994-1998", Lodz University, Lodz, processed.

Konings, Jozef, 1992, "Job creation and job destruction in the U.K.", Manufacturing Sector, April, London School of Economics and Political Science. Centre for Economic Performance, Discussion Paper No. 138: 1 – 4, unpublished manuscript.

Kupiszewski M., H.Durham, P.Rees, 1998, "Changes in the regional population dynamics in Poland 1980-1984". Studia Demograficzne 3/133, 3 – 18, Warsaw.

Kupiszewski M., Durham H., Rees P., 1998, "Internal migration and urban change in Poland", *European Journal of Population*, 14, 3, 265-290.

Layard, Richard, Stephen Nickell, and Richard Jackman, 1991, *Unemployment, Macroeconomic Performance and the Labour Market*, Oxford: Oxford University Press.

Martin, J., 2000, "What works among active labor market programs: evidence from OECD countries' experiences", OECD Economic Studies, Paris, June.

Nesporowa, Alena, 1999, "Employment and Labour Market Policies in Transition Economies", Geneva: ILO.

Newell, A. and B. Reilly, 1999, "Rates of return to educational qualifications in the transitional economies", *Education Economics*, 7(1): 67-84.

Newell A. and Socha M., 1998, "Wage distribution in Poland: the roles of privatization and international trade, 1992-96", *Economics of Transition*, Volume 6(1): 47 – 65

OECD (Organization for Economic Cooperation and Development), 1990, *OECD Employment Outlook*, Paris: OECD.

OECD (Organization for Economic Cooperation and Development), 1992, *Structural Change and Economic Performance: A Seven Country Growth Decomposition Study*, Paris: OECD.

OECD (Organization for Economic Cooperation and Development), 1999, *Employment Outlook*, Paris: OECD.

OECD (Organization for Economic Cooperation and Development), 2000, *Poland: 1999-2000 Annual Review*, Paris: OECD.

Okrasa, W., 1999, "The dynamics of poverty and the effectiveness of Poland's social safety net", World Bank Research Working Paper 2221, November. Washington, DC.

O'Leary J. Christopher, 1998, "Evaluating the Effectiveness of Active Labor Programs in Poland, Upjohn Institute Technical Report No. 98 – 012, June. Kalamazoo, Michigan.

Rutkowski J., 1996, "High skills pay off: the changing wage structure during economic transition in Poland", *Economics of Transition*, 4(1): 89-112.

Rutkowski J., 1996, "Changes in the wage structure during the transition in Poland", *Economics of Transition*, 4: 89 - 11

Rutkowski J., 2000, "The structural determinants of job creation: lessons from the regional analysis", mimeo, World Bank, Washington, DC.

Rutkowski, J., 2001, "Job Creation and Job Destruction in Poland: 1993-1999", mimeo, World Bank, Washington, DC.

Sapir, A. and D, Schumacher, 1985, "The employment impact of shift in the composition of commodity and services trade", In: *Employment Growth and Structural Change*, Paris: OECD.

Wood, A., 1991, "The factor content of North-South trade in manufactures reconsidered", *Weltwirtschaftliches Archiv*, 127: 719-743.

Wood, A, 1994, *North-South Trade, Employment and Inequality: Changing Fortunes in a Skill-Driven World*, Oxford: Clarendon Press.

World Bank, 2000, *Poland Trade and Foreign Direct Investment Study,* September 2000, Washington, DC.